PSYCHIATRY - THEORY, APPLICATIONS AND TREATMENTS

AFFECTIVE DISORDERS

EPIDEMIOLOGY, SIGNS/SYMPTOMS AND PROGNOSES

PSYCHIATRY - THEORY, APPLICATIONS AND TREATMENTS

Additional books in this series can be found on Nova's website under the Series tab.

Additional e-books in this series can be found on Nova's website under the e-book tab.

PSYCHIATRY - THEORY, APPLICATIONS AND TREATMENTS

AFFECTIVE DISORDERS

EPIDEMIOLOGY, SIGNS/SYMPTOMS AND PROGNOSES

LINDA D. HAMBRICK
EDITOR

NOVINKA

New York

For permission to use material from this book please contact us:
Telephone 631-231-7269; Fax 631-231-8175
Web Site: http://www.novapublishers.com

Library of Congress Cataloging-in-Publication Data

ISBN: 978-1-62618-402-2

Library of Congress Control Number: 2013935072

Published by Nova Science Publishers, Inc. † New York

CONTENTS

PREFACE

The affective spectrum is a grouping of related psychiatric and medical disorders which may accompany bipolar, unipolar, and schizoaffective disorders at statistically higher rates than would normally be expected. These disorders are identified by a common positive response to the same types of pharmacologic treatments. They also aggregate strongly in families and may therefore share common heritable underlying physiologic anomalies. In this book, the authors discuss the epidemiology, signs and symptoms, and prognoses of affective disorders. Topics include psychotic features in bipolar disorder; the risk of suicide behaviors in affective disorders; the social impact of major affective disorders; and gender differences in depressive prevalence in response to psychosocial issues.

Chapter 1 – Development of psychotic symptoms in bipolar disorder is frequent, particularly in the manic phases, when they are present in more than half cases. Paranoid delusions (followed by megalomaniac, ruin, hypochondriac, referential and bizarre delusions) and auditory hallucinations are the predominant psychotic symptoms. This appearance of psychotic symptoms is associated with a higher rate of family history of other psychotic disorders, higher comorbidity, worse clinical outcome and worse psychosocial adjustment. Some other studies have suggested that the development of psychotic symptoms could be associated with an early age at onset and alterations in the brain structure. Despite the above, there is a lack of specific vulnerability markers to predict the development of psychotic symptoms in the course of bipolar disorder. In the present chapter, original research on phenomenological description of psychosis through the different phases of bipolar disorder and external validators including family history, longitudinal course and treatment effects are reviewed.

Chapter 2 – Affective disorders and suicidal behaviors are closely linked. They are among the most important public health problems in the western world. One million people may die every year as a consequence of self-inflicted harm. Moreover, it is estimated that 9 to 36 million people attempt suicide every year. Within this population of suicide attempters, the prevalence of mental disorders is extremely high. The most frequent diagnosis among subjects who have completed suicide, according to psychological autopsies, is affective disorders. Specifically, bipolar disorder has been repeatedly reported as the mental disorder with the highest risk for completed suicide. In this chapter the author will analyze the current epidemiological data concerning the relationship between affective disorders and the suicidal spectrum, including suicidal ideation, attempted suicide and completed suicide. The author will also examine the association of affective disorders with specific subpopulations of suicide attempters, such as frequent attempters. In addition, the author will analyze the influence of sociodemographic and economic variables on the development of these types of behaviors. Finally, the author will introduce some of the available pharmacological treatment options and preventive strategies that have been applied to diminish the risk of suicidal behaviors among populations affected by affective disorders.

Chapter 3 – Mood disorders (MD) affect more than 5% of the general population determining significant functional impairment in sufferers and often leading to adverse social outcomes. MD include both the unipolar and bipolar types. Major depressive disorder is the most common affective disorder being one of the leading causes of premature death and disability among all diseases and accounting for enormous health service utilization. Comorbid anxiety and depression frequently co-exist and are associated with higher costs considering both individual and social perspectives. Patients with MD often present in primary care settings and require health care resources. Case identification and correct assessment are, no doubt, crucial in clinical practice. MD raise complicated challenges, often leading to inadequate diagnosis and treatment resulting in unnecessary patient distress and increased utilization of health care services. Providing an effective assessment, correct evaluation, and evidence-based treatment may improve quality of life in patients with MD. The author aimed to critically overview the current literature about MD, health effects, and social impact of these disabling conditions

Chapter 4 – Several lines of research suggest that the gender difference in depressive prevalence is due to the higher prevalence among women of a distinct depressive phenotype comprised of depression, disordered eating, body dissatisfaction, headaches, sleep problems, and fatigue that develops at adolescence. Furthermore, research shows that this phenotype is rooted in response to psychosocial issues particularly confronting contemporary women. First, women exhibit higher prevalence of all of these symptoms and, in all cases, the gender difference begins during adolescence as a result of dramatic increases in symptoms among females compared to males. Second, all of these somatic symptoms are more strongly related to depression among females than among males and this pattern too develops at adolescence. Third, all of these symptoms have been shown to have increased in prevalence over recent years among young women but not, or much less so, among men. Fourth, the variation among cohorts over the course of most of the twentieth century has been found to be similar between the gender difference in the prevalence of depression, the incidence of anorexia among young women, and the correlation between scores on depression inventories and the frequency of severe headache reported by women, three variables that would be expected to covary if a single disorder comprised of the symptoms discussed here afflicts women. These variations have been found to track historical changes in women's roles that probably led to an increase in the number of young women who were distressed by the limitations that had traditionally been placed on women. This suggests the possibility that the syndrome comprised of these symptoms might be rooted in psychosocial forces related to the dramatic changes in roles experienced by women in recent decades. Fifth, several studies have found that young women who report attitudes indicative of recognizing limitations placed upon them due to traditional gender roles, such as feeling that males have more opportunities than females or that their fathers exhibited preferences for males, exhibit high prevalence of depression accompanied by the additional symptoms listed above. Sixth, in self-report studies and large representative epidemiologic samples, this phenotype has been found to represent much of the higher prevalence of depression among women.

In: Affective Disorders
Editor: Linda D. Hambrick
ISBN: 978-1-62618-402-2

Chapter 1

PSYCHOTIC FEATURES IN BIPOLAR DISORDER

Guillermo Lahera*[*], *Patricia Hernández and Mariella Vilela
Department of Psychiatry, Príncipe de Asturias University Hospital, University of Alcalá, Madrid, Spain

ABSTRACT

Development of psychotic symptoms in bipolar disorder is frequent, particularly in the manic phases, when they are present in more than half cases. Paranoid delusions (followed by megalomaniac, ruin, hypochondriac, referential and bizarre delusions) and auditory hallucinations are the predominant psychotic symptoms. This appearance of psychotic symptoms is associated with a higher rate of family history of other psychotic disorders, higher comorbidity, worse clinical outcome and worse psychosocial adjustment. Some other studies have suggested that the development of psychotic symptoms could be associated with an early age at onset and alterations in the brain structure. Despite the above, there is a lack of specific vulnerability markers to predict the development of psychotic symptoms in the course of bipolar disorder. In the present chapter, original research on phenomenological description of psychosis through the different phases of bipolar disorder and external

* Corresponding author's email: guillermo.lahera@uah.es.

validators including family history, longitudinal course and treatment effects are reviewed.

1. Introduction

It is currently accepted that the development of psychotic symptoms is nonspecific of any diagnostic category, as they may appear in different mental disorders (from schizophrenia to Alzheimer disease, cocaine intoxication, bipolar disorder…). In addition, the Kraepelinian dichotomy regarding the onset, evolution and prognosis of *dementia praecox* and manic-depressive illness is increasingly challenged. There seems to be a large genetic and clinical overlap between the two entities. Thus, the Schneider´s *first-rank* symptoms can be found in both disorders. It has been observed also familial aggregation for the development of psychotic symptoms in both schizophrenia and bipolar disorder. The purpose of this chapter is to discuss the clinical relevance of psychotic symptoms in bipolar disorder and to detect what conditions are associated with their development.

More than half of patients with bipolar disorder experience psychotic symptoms in their lifetime (Dunayevich and Keck, 2000) and, in patients with bipolar mania, rates of psychotic symptoms as high as 68% have been reported (Pope and Lipinski, 1978; Coryell et al., 2001; Keck et al., 2003). All types of psychotic symptoms can occur in mania. However, certain types of symptoms, such as grandiose delusions (and persecutory ideas related to grandiosity), have been considered specifically characteristic of mania and the most common type of psychotic symptoms. Mood-incongruent or bizarre delusions, persistent auditory hallucinations, formal thought disorder, and catatonia can also present as part of a manic episode (Dunayevich and Keck, 2000; Potash et al., 2001; McElroy SL, Keck PE Jr, Strakowski SM, 1996). In a review of 26 studies of psychotic symptoms in mania, Goodwin and Jamison concluded that approximately 58% of patients with bipolar disorder had a lifetime history of at least one psychotic symptom, usually when manic. It has been estimated that 48% of patients experiencing a manic episode present with at least one delusion, 19% with one thought disorder and 15% with one hallucination (Goodwin and Jamison, 1990). In the Finnish study JoBs (Jorvi Bipolar Group) that included 191 patients diagnosed of bipolar disorder; authors found that frequency of lifetime psychotic features reaches 50% of the cases, twice as often in bipolar I than in bipolar II (bipolar I 67,8% vs. bipolar II 33,7%). Also, many lifetime psychotic bipolar I patients had had at least one episode of mania (67.2%) or depression (36%) (Mantere et al, 2004). Other studies in patients with acute manic or mixed episodes in patients with bipolar disorder type 1 support the previous results, indicating high rates of psychotic features in patients with bipolar mania (Canuso et al., 2008). Grandiosity, delusions, lack of judgment/insight, excitement, suspiciousness/persecution and hostility were PANSS items with the highest scores. Excitement and hostility are characteristic of mania which explains high PANSS scores but they are not defined by a psychotic dimension according to the PANSS User's Manual (Kay et al., 2000). Grandiosity, delusions, lack of judgment/insight and suspiciousness/persecution have a delusional/hallucinatory component at some PANSS severity rating which suggests they are the most prevalent symptoms of psychosis in bipolar mania. Canuso et al. found that PANSS and also YMRS scores at baseline were significantly higher in patients with psychotic features than in patients without psychotic features and GAF scores were significantly lower suggesting that psychosis is associated with generally more severe illness according to several measures (Swann et al., 2004).

In summary, psychosis may be even more common in bipolar patients than is typically diagnosed, so its recognition and treatment are important components in the effective management of these patients.

2. Prevalence and Phenomenology of Psychotic Symptoms in Bipolar Disorder

Psychotic symptoms in BD include hallucinations, delusions and disorganization. Between 35% and 60% of manic episodes were accompanied by grandiose delusions, 18% to 65% by persecutory delusions, 7% to 48% experienced auditory hallucinations, and 9% to 34% experienced Schneiderian first-rank symptoms These psychotic features tend to be brief, intermittent, fragmented and often related to religious themes. Patients experience them especially when they are alone and typically with an absolute lack of insight (however, when psychotic symptoms remit, the insight appears and patients usually explain the experience as a transient mental disorder). Delusions and hallucinations usually disappear early during recovery from a manic episode but are more persistent in psychotic depression; in both cases, they are more pronounced in severe affective states. The delusions accompanying mania are often short-lived and changeable, poorly systematized, and often have grandiose, religious, or paranoid content, being less fixed than in schizophrenia or paranoia (Lahera et al, 2006). Some authors have compared the phenomenology of psychotic symptoms in BD to these experienced in toxic psychosis (specially induced by pro-dopaminergic and stimulant agents). Overall, delusions occur up to three times more frequently than hallucinations (Goodwin and Jamison, 1990; Lowe GR, 1973; Winokur G, Clayton PJ, Reich T, 1969; Carlson GA, Goodwin FK, 1973; Goodwin DW, Alderson P, Rosenthal R, 1971).

Psychotic symptoms are more frequent in bipolar than unipolar depression. Parker et al. (2000), in a sample of 83 bipolar and 904 unipolar depressed patients, established that those with bipolar depression were more likely to have delusions and hallucinations, with odds ratios suggesting a two-fold greater chance (Parker et al., 2000). In other study, 25 % of 1703 bipolar I patients developed psychotic features during an episode of depression. This was significantly higher (up to five times) than the prevalence of psychotic symptoms in patients with recurrent major depression (6 % prevalence of psychotic features from 2487 subjects (Goes et al., 2007). Then, presence of psychotic symptoms during a major depressive episode increases probability of diagnosis of bipolar disorder. In a recently research, Tohen et al. (2012) completed a two-year follow-up of 49 patients after first acute episode of mayor depressive disorder with psychotic features. Among the 49 subjects, 20 (40.8%) changed diagnosis to bipolar disorder (type I or NOS 70.0%) or to schizoaffective disorder (30.0%). Changes to bipolar disorder were significantly associated with mood-lability and subsyndromal hypomanic symptoms (insufficient to meet DSM IV criteria for a mixed episode); whereas changes associated with schizoaffective disorders were: presence of any Schneiderian first-rank psychotic symptoms and presence of first-episode formal thought disorder. These findings support the association between psychotic symptoms and subsequent development of bipolar disorder, as well as that the identification of mixed features in patients with psychotic depression may have important implications in terms of outcome (Tohen et al., 2012).

The key clinical characteristics for the diagnosis of bipolar depression - described by some authors as the "signature" of those episodes are: psychomotor retardation; melancholic features as worthlessness and marked anhedonia, atypical symptoms such as hypersomnia and leaden paralysis, presence of psychotic symptoms, and lack of anxiety, conciliation insomnia or tearfulness (Mitchell and Malhi, 2004; Mitchell et al., 2008; Perlis et al., 2006; Goodwin et al., 2008). Some authors have failed to find real clinical differences between bipolar and unipolar depression. In a study with 70 psychotic depressed outpatients, bipolar and unipolar psychotic depression were compared in age, duration of illness, severity, recurrences, atypical features, chronicity, gender, comorbidity, hallucinations and delusions. The analysis did not find any significant differences between these indicators. Bipolar psychotic depression was more similar to unipolar psychotic depression than to non-psychotic bipolar depression. In this regard, authors suggested that psychotic depression could be a distinct clinical entity (Benazzi F, 1999a). Subsequently these findings have been interpreted by others as evidence of the close link between psychotic depression and bipolar disorder.

In the study by Ostergaard et al. (2012), that include 14 529 patients with a diagnosis of bipolar disorder, a lifetime incidence of psychotic depression of 15% was found. These patients who experience psychotic symptoms during a depressive episode were more likely to have also psychotic symptoms in the manic episode, and that there was a greater occurrence of mixed episodes in patients with a history of psychotic mania and / or depression.

The presence of psychotic symptoms in bipolar II disorder is not rare, although compared with bipolar I disorder, type II presents psychotic symptoms less frequently. This can be attributed to the fact that bipolar II disorder, by definition, does not experience psychotic symptoms during episodes of mood elevation, while in bipolar I disorder about half of patients present with psychotic mania. It has also been found that psychotic features in bipolar depression are less common in type II than type I (Goodwin et al., 2008; Benazzi F, 1999b; Ketter et al., 2004). Benazzi (1999b) with a total of 235 patients with bipolar depression (59 with a history of psychotic depressive episode, 176 with history only of non-psychotic depressive episode), found that 77.9% of psychotics had a diagnosis of bipolar disorder type I, while than in non-psychotic predominated type II bipolar disorder (94.3%) (Benazzi F, 1999b). Specifically, in bipolar II disorder psychotic symptoms over time occur in a range between 3 and 45% of patients. The wide variability of these rates is justified by the lack of research and because methodological and demographic differences between existing studies (Mazzarini et al., 2010). Patients with BD type II and a history of psychotic symptoms were older in age than those without psychotic episodes, but, as in bipolar I disorder, were less likely to have a family history of bipolar disorder (Mazzarini et al., 2010).

Psychotic symptoms in pediatric bipolar disorder have been also examined. Tillman et al (2008) indicate that grandiose delusions were the most common type of delusions and visual hallucinations were the most prevalent hallucinations. In contrast, Hua et al. (2011), Pavuluri et al. (2005), and Ulloa et al (2000) have found that auditory hallucinations were the most common hallucinations. They also found that grandiosity and persecutory delusions had similar rates in their sample. But there is an agreement regarding the close relation between bipolar episodes and psychotic symptoms during the childhood and adolescence. Longitudinal studies found that those affective patients who further develop bipolar disorder were more likely to have psychotic symptoms and psychomotor slowing at the onset episode (Strober et al., 1993). Thus, we can affirm that a depressive episode with psychotic symptoms, at any age, should raise the suspicion of a diagnosis of bipolar disorder (Goodwin et al., 2008).

Since Bleuler (1911), we know that disorders of thought (and thus, speech) and content (delusions) should be considered separately. Circumstantiality, tangentiality, pressure of speech, distractibility, loosening of associations, incoherence, neologisms, blocking, poverty of content of speech, perseveration, echolalia, clanging, derailment, illogical thoughts are examples of formal thougth disorder. Andreasen (1979) differentiated positive (pressure of speech, racing thoughts, derailment, loss of goal, tangentiality, distractibility and over inclusive thinking) and negative types of thought disorder (poverty of speech, disorganized speech, neologisms, private use of words and under inclusive thinking), and prevalence differences between positive and negative types (less frequently) in manic patients were observed. Although thought disorders appear in mania and schizophrenia with comparable rates (McElroy et al, 1996), several findings suggest qualitative differences between manic and schizophrenic thought disorder, whereas some authors considered an overlap (Abrams and Taylor, 1981). Thought disorder in manic patients may be associated with pressured speech (Kufferle B, Lenz G, Schanda H, 1985) and may have a less consistent presentation in subsequent admissions than in schizophrenic subjects (Earle-Boyer et al., 1986). Manic patients tend to have more combinatory and over inclusive thinking, merging ideas and precepts, whereas schizophrenic thought disorder tends to be more disorganized, more bizarre and less playful.

Psychotic symptoms in BD can be classified as mood congruent and incongruent. Mood-congruent psychotic symptoms include delusions and hallucinations whose content is consistent with manic or depressive themes, such as inflated worth, power, knowledge, identity, or special relationship to a deity or famous person. Patients who present elation, energy and grandiosity (common features of mania) may feel that they can communicate with God or experience divine messages (Akiskal and Puzantian, 1979). Although this may technically be a Schneiderian first-rank symptom, Akiskal and Puzantian (1979) conceptualized it as a mood-congruent psychotic symptom. Thus, depressive patients who present low self-esteem, sadness and absolute lack of interest in enjoyable activities may develop delusional guilt, feeling of self-negation (nihilistic or Cotard syndrome) or the conviction of being ruined. Mood-incongruent psychotic symptoms include persecutory ideas unrelated to manic themes, such as persecutory delusions not directly related to grandiose ideas or themes, thought diffusion or insertion, and delusions of being controlled.

Studies about the differences of psychotic symptoms prevalence depending on the congruence with the mood state are controversial. Tohen et al (1992) found that mood-incongruent psychotic features were more frequent (56% of subjects) than mood congruent features (44%) in mania patients. In this study, paranoid ideation (includes both mood-congruent and mood-incongruent) was present in 65% of the sample, first-rank symptoms in 20%, bizarre delusions in 17%, auditory hallucinations in 30% and visual hallucinations in 9%. Fennig et al (1996) reported similar frequency of mood-congruent (24%) and mood-incongruent (20%) psychotic symptoms in manic patients. Finally, Toni et al (2001) found that 55 % of manic patients presented incongruent psychotic symptoms. Authors tried to clarify the significance of these symptoms on the course and clinical presentation of mania and define the specific characteristics associated with incongruent manic psicosis. They did not found differences in demographic and clinical characteristics (index age, age at onset, age at first treatment, polarity of the first episode, number of total episodes, presence of hypomania, pharmacologic hypomania and affective temperament) when comparing this group to manic patients without mood- incongruent psychotic symptoms. These findings were in agreement with most observations (Young et al., 1983; Fennig et al., 1996). Although some studies have reported a correlation between early age at onset and further development of psychotic symptoms (Carlson and Strober, 1979; Rosenthal et al., 1980; Rosen et al., 1983; McGlashan, 1988; De Heredia et al, 2001), most results have not confirmed this relationship (McElroy et al., 1997; Sax et al., 1997; Perugi et al., 2000). Toni et al also observed some special characteristics in patients with mood-incongruent psychotic features that may be indicators of severity and chronicity such as longer duration of the current episode, higher percentage of chronic course, more suicide attempts and hospitalizations. These findings are consistent with most of the previous literature (Tohen et al., 1990; Coryell et al., 1990; Perugi et al., 1999).

Kendler (1991) concluded that mood-incongruent mood disorder is a distinct subtype of affective illness, and longitudinal studies have found that bipolar patients with mood-incongruent psychotic features has significantly worse psychosocial outcome and illness course (Brockington et al., 1983; De Leon et al., 2000), more severe positive and negative psychotic symptoms and poorer social adjustment (Miklowitz, 1992), greater prevalence of psychosis, poorer overall functioning (Strakowski et al., 2000), lower Global Assessment of Functioning (GAF) scores and shorter time in remission (Tohen et al. 1992) than bipolar patients with mood-congruent psychosis. Azorin et al. (2007) observed that 50% of manic patients had psychotic symptoms (mood-congruent psychotic features were the most common). Patients with mood-incongruent psychotic symptoms were more likely to have less interepisodic remission, greater mood instability, poor course due to paranoid elaborations and tend to be misdiagnosed as schizophrenic. In contrast with this, Keck et al., (2003) reported that a history of mood-incongruent psychosis was not associated with significant differences in psychosocial, vocational or clinical outcome compared with a history of mood-congruent psychosis. An explanation for this controversial result may be the relatively high morbidity and poor functional outcome of a substantial portion of the total sample. Toni et al. (2001) observed that mood-incongruent psychotic (MIP) patients scored higher on auditory hallucinations, persecutory delusions, delusions of reference, somatic delusions and aggressive-agitated behavior. Furthermore, mood-congruent psychotic patients showed higher scores on grandiose and religious delusions, and clanging and distractible speech. Finally, it should be noted that mood-incongruence psychotic symptoms often lead to misdiagnosis. In a Spanish study was found that an unstable diagnosis was not associated with demographic variables but with mood incongruent psychotic symptoms during first bipolar disorder episode (Gonzalez-Pinto et al., 1998).

Catatonic symptoms include motor abnormalities such as immobility, negativism, mutism, echolalia, echopraxia, or excessive motor activity (DSM-IVTR). Abrams and Taylor (1976) observed that catatonic symptoms are more frequently present in patients with affective disorders (28% of acutely manic patients displayed at least one catatonic sign) than in patients with psychotic disorders, suggesting that these symptoms are nonspecific for diagnosis. Bräunig et al (1998) concluded that catatonic symptoms are a marker of a more severe outcome in mania (related to the presence of mixed episodes, severe manic symptoms, more general psychopathology, longer hospital stays, higher prevalence of comorbidity and lower Global Assessment of Functioning (GAF) scores.

Discussion about the boundaries between bipolar illness and other psychotic disorders has been addressed (Blacker and Tsuang, 1992). *Postpartum psychosis* is associated with affective illness in up to 57% of cases. It may present severe mood-incongruent psychotic symptoms (Oosthuizen P et al., 1995) and, through the time, about one third of total cases are diagnosed as bipolar disorder (Schopf and Rust, 1994). Prophylactic treatment with lithium is associated with a decrease in relapse rate, suggesting again a clear relationship between postpartum psychosis and bipolar disorder (Cohen et al., 1995; Austin et al., 1992; Stewart et al., 1991). *Cycloid psychoses* syndromes were classified by Leonhard (1999) into three subforms: anxiety-happiness psychosis, excited-inhibited psychosis, and hyperkinetic-akinetic psychosis. They are characterized by delusions (paranoid ideation, ideas of reference), hallucinations (acoustic, visual or tactile or cenestesic), formal thought disorder (distractibility, incoherence), confusion, psychomotor agitation or retardation and affective symptoms (ecstatic and elevated mood), characteristically with complete recovery from each phase. Their relationship to affective illness has been the subject of debate for many years. While some European researchers understand cycloid psychoses as separate diagnostic entities (Beckmann et al., Maj M. 1990), others think that they are best understood as atypical varieties of affective psychosis (Cutting, 1990). *Periodic catatonia* is a recurrent psychotic syndrome that may or may not be presented with affective symptoms. It also has good prognosis with good response to pharmacological treatment (Petursson; Wald et al., 1976).

One current object of discussion is if psychotic episodes of bipolar I and II disorder are just more severe clinical manifestations or if they represent different biological subtypes of the illness (Potash et al., 2001). Studies with bipolar I patients have found that those who had never developed psychotic symptoms have more family history of bipolar disorder in comparison with the bipolar psychotic patients. These findings support the assumption of a non-psychotic and primarily affective bipolar disorder phenotype (Keck et al., 2003). In the same way, Potash et al. (2001) with studies of familial aggregation in bipolar disorder, found more family background of psychotic episodes in bipolar psychotic patients in comparison with non psychotic bipolar cases (Potash et al., 2001). Also, twin studies suggest that schizophrenia diagnosis in one twin increases risk for both schizophrenia and affective psychosis in the co-twin (Cardno et al., 2002). With these evidences, Potash et al. (2003) considered that psychotic features in bipolar disorder would be a phenotypic manifestation of common genes between bipolar disorder and schizophrenia. Genomic studies found out cromosomal loci that may influence in susceptibility to psychotic episodes regardless of diagnostic categories. Detailed studies of linked genomic regions have identified several putative candidate genes which appear to be involved in schizophrenia and affective psychoses: NRG 1, DTNBP1, DISC 1, COMT, G72/G30, BDNF, and RGS 4 (Ivleva et al., 2008). From de point of view of the authors that stand up for the conception of the mayor psychosis in a dimensional better than a categorical model, affective psychosis is worse in severity than non psychotic affective disorders, but less severe than schizophrenia. And, if this conception is linked with the existence of shared genetic vulnerability, it can be considered that earlier development of psychosis features in a patient would be related to more genetic susceptibility and worse prognosis. Congruently with this postulate, studies have detected more prevalence of psychotic symptoms in patients with earlier onset of bipolar disorder in comparison with those who developed later the disease (Ketter et al., 2004)

Historically, failure to return to baseline functioning after a psychotic episode has been taken as a mayor distinction between schizophrenia and affective psychosis. However, some studies described that almost 20-25% of patients with bipolar disorder have several difficulties and considerable long-term impairment in daily functioning (Goldberg and Harrow, 2004).

3. Clinical Factors Associated with the Development of Psychotic Symptoms in Bipolar Disorder

Some clinical factors of the BD have been proposed as specifically linked to the development of psychotic symptoms. Next we exposed the empirical data that support each potential association:

3.1. Family History of Psychotic Disorder

Studies addressing the potential association between family history of psychosis (such as schizophrenia, chronic delusional disorder or acute psychotic disorder) and development of psychotic symptoms in BD have been contradictory, but, overall, they show empirical basis for this link. Mendlewicz et al. (1972) found that bipolar patients with a family history of affective illness had more frequent psychotic symptoms during mania. Abrams and Taylor (1981) noted that this association was stronger in manic patients who presented more schizophrenic-like features. Endicott et al. (1986) found that bipolar disorder and psychosis were positively associated in both probands and relatives. Hua et al. (2011) found higher rates of family history of psychosis in children and adolescents with psychotic bipolar disorder compared with non-psychotic bipolar disorder. Other studies have inversely found increased rates of bipolar disorder with psychotic symptoms in relatives of psychotic patients such as schizoaffective ones, especially when the probands have the manic or bipolar subtype of the disorder (Andreasen et al., 1987; Maier et al., 1992; Kendler et al., 1993). A larger study (Potash et al., 2001) compared the rates of psychotic symptoms in 202 first-degree relatives of 47 psychotic and 18 non-psychotic bipolar patients. Those researchers found that 64% of families of the psychotic patients had at least one relative who had affective disorder with psychotic symptoms, whereas 28% of non-psychotic probands had at least one relative who had affective disorder with psychotic symptoms. Additionally, 34% of affectively ill relatives of psychotic probands had psychotic symptoms, versus 11% of nonpsychotic probands. Authors concluded that hallucinations and delusions during affective episodes have familial aggregation in bipolar disorder pedigrees. An Spanish epidemiological study, with 103 bipolar patients and 84 healthy controls, found results that suggest a non-specific transmission of psychosis, regardless diagnostic categories (Vallés et al, 2000).

Negative results towards this association were reported by Winokur et al. (1995), who compared psychosis rates among relatives of 30 bipolar patients. In contrast, Keck et al. (2003), in a sample of bipolar I patients, found that family history of bipolar disorder were more commonly among patients without a history of psicosis, which may represent the transmission of a primarily affective, non- psychotic phenotype of bipolar illness.

3.2. Suicide Risk

Bipolar disorder has a high risk of completed suicide, which is associated with a history of suicide attempts, and it is specially increased in patients who are in the depressed phase, who have mixed states, or who have psychotic mania (Simpson and Jamison, 1999). Lifetime rates of suicide attempt among BD patients range from 20% to 56% in different studies. In adults, the specific risk associated with the presence of psychotic symptoms is unclear, given that some studies have found an increased suicidal behavior (Axelsson et al, 1992) and others have not (Keck et al, 2003; Black D et al., 1988). Toni et al (2000) showed that this association was only valid for mood-incongruent psychotic symptoms.

Oquendo et al. (2000) suggested that psychotic symptoms may impair the ability to plan and execute suicide attempts. They reported a trend towards a lower rate of positive psychotic symptoms in suicide attempters than non-attempters. In this line, Azorin et al. (2009) found fewer psychotic symptoms in manic BD-I inpatients with a history of suicide attempt than nonattempters. With these findings, it has been suggested that psychosis may impair planning for suicide attempts. Slama et al (2004) identified some clinical characteristics of bipolar patients at risk of suicide: early age at bipolar disorder onset, high number of depressive episodes, personal history of antidepressant-induced mania, comorbid alcohol abuse, and previous suicidal behavior. The development of psychosis did not appear as a relevant factor. Similarly, the study of López et al (2001) investigated the association between suicide attempts and the predictive factors previously described in the literature. Drug abuse, family history of affective disorders and severe depressive episodes – and not the presence of psychotic symptoms- were the factors with strongest relation. Another negative finding was reported by Johnson et al. (2005), who founded similar incidences of psychotic symptoms in suicide attempters and non-attempters with bipolar I disorder. Even, Grunebaum et al. (2001) found that patients with bipolar disorder who had delusions on admission had lower suicidal ideation during the prior 2 weeks than those without delusions. It seems that –at least- grandiose delusions may have a protective effect. Suicidality is mostly related to hopelessness and meaninglessness, and delusion may be a source of (aberrant) meaning. This hypothetical protective role against suicide is balanced with the extreme emotions and anguish induced by most of delusions, which provokes an increase of impulsive and disorganized behavior.

Among the studies that show a positive association between suicide risk and psychotic symptoms in BD, highlights the recent findings by Song et al. (2012). They also examined the characteristics of bipolar disorder patients with and without a history of suicide attempts to identify the risk factors of suicide. They found an association between suicide risk and younger age at onset, history of antidepressant use and lifetime history of auditory hallucinations. Specially, a history of depressive episodes with psychotic symptoms predicted the first suicide attempt in patients with bipolar disorder. An association between the presence of psychotic symptoms and a higher prevalence of suicidal ideation and planning has been also reported in pediatric patients with bipolar disorder (Caetano et al., 2006; Goldstein et al., 2005; Papolos et al., 2005). Goldstein et al. (2005) examined the factors that may increase the risk for suicide attempt in pediatric bipolar disorder, and the results were: history of mixed episodes, BP-I, comorbid substance use, panic disorder, non-suicidal self-injurious behavior, family history of suicide attempt, history of hospitalization and history of physical and/or sexual abuse, and psychotic features.

3.3. Gender

There are again mixed findings supporting a potential link between gender and development of psychotic symptoms, what is partially explained by methodological differences across studies. Recently, Braunig et al. (2009) examined gender differences in the prevalence and types of psychotic symptoms in bipolar mania. They assessed 137 women and 109 men with an acute manic episode, of whom 93 women and 62 men had psychotic symptoms. Results showed that women had more delusions and hallucinations than men, with more paranoid delusions and ideas of reference. Despite clinical characteristics of nonpsychotic men and women were generally similar, psychotic women had a more severe index episode (measured by YMRS score) and more previous episodes of depression compared with psychotic men and nonpsychotic women with mania. Interestingly, differences in marital status were also found; women with psychotic mania were more often single or divorced compared with men. However, other studies (Hendrick et al., 2000; Benazzi F, 1999) have not found a gender difference in the number of psychotic affective episodes.

In summary we do not have enough evidence to claim that the development of psychotic symptoms in BD is one of the gender-related clinical factors. Until now, data show that manic episodes are more common in men and depressive episodes occur more frequently in women; and that women have a higher probability of experiencing mixed episodes and greater comorbidity of physical pathology, particularly thyroid diseases (Vega et al, 2011).

3.4. Severity of Manic Symptoms

Carlson and Goodwin (1973) reported that as core manic symptoms increased in severity during an acute episode, psychotic symptoms became more common, prominent and bizarre. Increased severity of manic symptoms, earlier age of onset and adolescent presentation are more likely to be associated with psychotic symptoms (Carlson et Goodwin, 1973; Carlson et al, 2000; Young et al., 1978). Beyond episode severity, Azorin et al. (2007) examine different factors that may contribute to psychosis in mania. According to previous studies, they concluded that increase in severity of manic symptoms increases the likelihood of psychotic symptoms which support the DSM-IV conception according to which mania with psychotic symptoms may be considered as a severe episode. Nevertheless, other features may be considered as precursors or risk factors for psychotic mania: younger index age, comorbid social phobia and single marital status.

3.5. Age of Onset

As it occurs in schizophrenia, an early age at BD onset is related to more symptom severity and poorer prognosis. Carlson and Strober (1979) found that adolescent onset was characterized by florid psychotic symptoms. Rosenthal (1980) observed that bipolar I patients who also met Research Diagnostic Criteria for schizoaffective illness had a younger age of onset and more non-Schneiderian delusions and hallucinations. Rosen et al (1983) found a negative correlation between age at onset and psychotic symptoms score, and McGlashan (1988) found that adolescent-onset patients displayed significantly more delusions and hallucinations than adult-onset patients. Carlson (2000) showed that earlier age of onset (between 15 and 20 years) was associated with paranoid ideation in 100% of the sample and grandiosity in 74%, as compared with 80% and 74% respectively in the adult-onset group. Research groups have found that one-fifth of youths meeting diagnostic criteria for BP I will also have hallucinations or delusions during the course of a mood episode (Kowatch RA et al,. 2005).

In contrast with these previous results, a significantly lower rate of psychotic features was found in adolescents compared to adults (McElroy et al., 1997) and early versus late onset manic patients (Sax et al., 1997).

3.6. Race

Several studies have examined racial differences in bipolar symptomatology. Studies have reported increased frequency and severity of hallucinations, paranoia and other psychotic symptoms in African-American compared to Caucasian patients (Adebimpe et al., 1982; Helzer, 1975; Mukherjee et al., 1983).

Strakowski et al (1995) reported that increased rates of first-rank symptoms of schizophrenia in African-American patients were associated with over-diagnosed for schizophrenia, even with similar rates or current manic and depressive syndromes. Strakowski et al (1996) examines racial differences in diagnosis and symptoms expression in a sample of manic patients with psychotic features. Over 20% of these patients exhibited one or more first-rank symptoms, adding to the literature that these symptoms are not specific for schizophrenia (Goodwin and Jameson, 1990). African-American patients with psychotic mania have higher rates of schizophrenia diagnoses than bipolar or schizoaffective disorder compared with Caucasian. Psychotic symptoms in African Americans (mainly auditory hallucinations, persecutory delusions, and delusions of inference) tend to be more severe compared with Caucasians (Kennedy et al., 2004; Strakowski et al., 1996; Van Os et al., 1996) which may contribute to poor recovery among African Americans.

Kennedy et al. (2004) found that African Americans usually have earlier onset of mania compared with whites, and whites were more likely to present a depressive episode before mania (Kennedy et al., 2004). Other studies have examined whether Latinos are more or less likely to present psychotic symptoms, with mixed results (Vega et al., 2007). Minsky et al. (2003) found that Latinos were more likely to present with depressive symptoms than whites.

Recently, Gonzalez JM et al (2010) found that depression response to treatment was slower among African Americans with psychotic symptoms than among African Americans without psychotic symptoms and among non-Hispanic whites with or without psychotic symptoms. No differences between Hispanics and non-Hispanic whites in response times and recovery were observed.

3.7. Personality

Several studies have been carried out regarding the complex relationship and bidirectional interactions between personality and affective disorders. Up to now, it is not possible to associate a specific personality with the development of psychotic symptoms in bipolar disorder. Personality has been historically considered a vulnerability factor or a behavioral marker for bipolar disorder (Kraepelin, 1976; Angst, 2000). Kraepelin noted that individuals who develop mood disorders, which can range from the most severe forms of psychotic mania to milder forms of depression, are expressed from the underlying personality traits, genetically determined, called affective temperaments.

Kraepelin (1921) described four personality variants: the hyperthymic type associated with unipolar mania; a cyclothymic type associated with mania and depresión; an irritable type associated with atypical depresión and the depressive type associated with unipolar depression). The existence of these temperaments has led to personality models based on affective spectrum expressions (Akiskal, 1983).

Akiskal notifies the diagnostic trouble when a bipolar disorder occurs in a "wrong" personality, (eg schizoid), in which social withdrawal predominates. He suggested that personality may shape the clinical presentation or outcome of affective disorders and that personality may be modified by repeated mood episodes.

The Temperament and Character Inventory (TCI) has been used to evaluate different components of personality in several studies. The TCI (Cloninger et al., 1993) distinguish four temperament (novelty seeking, harm avoidance, reward dependence and persistence) and three character dimensions (self-directedness (responsable, goal-directed/insecure, inept), cooperativeness (helpful, empathic/hostile, aggresive) and self-transcendence (imaginative, unconventional/ controlling, materialistic)). Cloninger et al (1998), who studied 804 adult subjects representative of the general population, found associations between traits (measured by the Temperament and Character Inventory) and affective disorders. Higher scores on three dimensions of temperamento have been found in different studies: harm avoidance (Young et al., 1995; Osher et al., 1996; Hirano et al., 2002; Engstrom et al., 2004; Evans et al., 2005), novelty seeking (Young et al., 1995; Osher et al., 1999; Evans et al., 2005), and reward dependence (Osher et al., 1996),: However, lower scores on persistence (Osher et al., 1996; Osher et al., 1999) and self-directedness (Engstrom et al., 2004a; Evans et al., 2005). Engstrom et al (2003) associated higher scores on harm avoidance with early onset of disease and fewer suicide attempts in bipolar disorder.

Patients with bipolar psychosis get high scores on the trait cooperativeness and self-transcendence (Goodwin and Jamison, 1990), which are characteristic of schizotypal, ciclothymic or paranoid personalities. Blairy et al. (2000); Rogers et al. (2004) and Staner et al. (1998) suggested that bipolar disorder and personality traits may share a common familial or genetic predisposition.

Nevertheless, none of these associations has a definite strength and remains to be clarified whether psychopathology creates personality differences, or vice versa.

3.8. Outcome and Prognosis

The presence of psychotic symptoms during manic episodes has been associated with negative long-term prognostic with lower therapeutic response (Young et al., 1983; Rosen et al., 1983a; Tohen et al., 1992). Poor treatment outcome has been specially related to the presence of hallucinations (Taylor and Abrams, 1975), persecutory delusions (Beigel and Murphy, 1971; Murphy and Beigel, 1974; Taylor and Abrams, 1975) and formal thought disorder (Tohen et al., 1992). Other studies have linked psychosis in mania with clinical severity, lower frequency of rapid cycling and higher level of social impairment (Sato et al, 2002; Swann et al, 2001). However, the relevance of psychotic symptoms on delineating the evolution of manic depressive illness has not been uniformly and definitely defined. It is not still clear if they represent a state or trait related phenomena or they identify a different nosological subcategory. For example, in a review of six long-term studies that examined the prognostic significance of psychosis in patients with bipolar disorder, Keck et al. (2003) found a wide range of positive and negative outcomes, concluding that the results were inconclusive regarding the general prognostic impact of psychotic features in bipolar patients.

Although some studies report psychotic symptoms associated with longer hospitalizations (Kessing, 2004), more time ill (Geller et al., 2004), overall impairment (Haro et al., 2006), increased recurrence (Tohen et al., 2003), greater symptom severity and higher morbidity in the long-term (Coryell et al., 2001), other studies reported a lack of prognostic relevance (Keck et al., 2003; Goldberg and Harrow, 2004).

Thus, researchers have reported a variety of conflicting results between psychosis and outcomes, including that psychotic features are predictive of worse psychosocial outcome (Rosen et al., 1983a; Tohen et al., 1990) but they are linked to decreased rates of relapse during lithium maintenance therapy (Rosenthal et al., 1979). At the same time, others have found no relationship between psychosis and any long-term outcomes (Goldberg et al., 1995; Harrow et al., 1990; Judd et al., 2002).

The prognostic implications of psychotic features in BD have been studied along the years. Pease (1912) found that the presence of hallucinations during manic episodes predicted more rapid short-term recovery. In contrast, Lundquist (1945) found that hallucinations during manic episodes had no prognostic significance, although the duration of manic episodes was significantly shorter in patients with confusion. However, for young patients with bipolar depression, the presence of delusions was associated with twice length of the episode. Rosen et al. (1983a) observed worse outcome in social functioning in patients with psychosis during an index mood episode. Winokur et al. (1985) reported that patients with psychosis were more likely to have had no prior mood episodes and the main symptom was tearfulness. Considering this result, authors suggested that bipolar patients with psychosis were more likely to have mixed episodes than those without. There were also trends for bipolar patients with psychosis to be less likely to be in remission at the time of hospital discharge and more likely to be chronically ill on follow-up. Tohen et al. (1990) in a four year follow-up study observed that patients with psychotic mania had a shorter time to recurrence after the index episode (up to 12 months) and a poor long-term outcome (after 12 to 48 months).

Harrow et al. (1990) followed 73 patients hospitalized for a bipolar manic episode for up to 1.7 years. The presence of psychotic symptoms did not predict outcome, although the overall outcome of the total cohort was poor. Goldberg et al. (1995) extended the follow-up of this cohort to 4.5 years, and there continued to be no significant difference in outcome between psychotic and nonpsychotic bipolar patients. The results of these two studies are inconclusive regarding the general prognostic impact of psychotic features in patients with bipolar disorder.

Coryell et al (2001) reported that psychotic symptoms in mania are associated with greater symptom severity and more long-term morbidity. Interestingly, psychotic features appear to be much less predictive of future psychosis when they occur within a manic episode than when they occur within a depressive episode. Tohen et al (2003) found that mood-congruent psychotic features and previous low occupational status were significant predictors of a new episode of mania.

In addition, bipolar subjects with psychotic symptoms or high number of previous depressive episodes are prone to experience subsyndromal long term depressive symptoms (Treuer and Tohen, 2010). Regarding this, Torrent et al. (2012), in their study of long-term outcome of cognitive impairment in bipolar disorder, have indicated that baseline subdepressive symptoms are associated with poor performance in executive function and subdepressive symptoms at endpoint are associated with poor functioning and therefore a worse long-term prognosis of bipolar patients. It has also been found that bipolar II patients with history of psychotic features show a greater number of hospitalizations. This is justified because psychotic symptoms often lead to impaired judgment and therefore tendency to life-threatening behaviors (Mazzarini et al., 2010).

3.9. Insight

Insight may be impaired in BD and it may play a role in compliance and course of illness (González-Pinto et al, 2010). It is a complex multidimensional phenomenon, and includes awareness of illness, awareness of symptoms, and the perceived need for treatment (David, 1990; Amador et al., 1993). The lack of insight in BD is state dependent (Ghaemi and Rosenquist 2004) and especially common among patients with manic episode. Dell'Osso et al. (2002) found that patients with mania had poorer insight into various aspects of their illness compared with patients with mixed mania, bipolar depression and unipolar depression. However, in this study, poor insight in mania group was not related to the number or severity of manic symptoms. Insight impacts on clinical course of the illness (e.g recognition of early warning signs of relapse), treatment compliance and psychosocial and functional outcomes. Fifty years ago, Jaspers et al (1963) report that both lack of insight (wrong ideas about the illness) and presence of delusions reflect a disconnect form reality which may involve an overlapping between pathological processes. Some studies have demonstrated a relationship between the severity of manic symptoms (including the development of delusions and hallucinations) and lack of insight (Copeland et al 2008). GüÇlü et al. (2011) have recently presented data supporting the idea that psychotic symptoms, especially delusions, rather than the severity of mania is related to lack of insight, which is consistent with the previous literature (Michalakeas et al. 1994, Weiler et al. 2000). Michalakeas et al (1994) and Fennig et al (1996) also suggested that the presence and the severity of psychotic symptoms is strongly correlated with lack of insight. Albus et al (1996) found an association between psychotic symptoms and cognitive performance, and between cognitive impaiment and lack of insight. In this line, Dickerson et al. (1997) and Debowska et al. (1998) also linked insight with delusions. Peralta and Cuesta (1998) reported more severe insight impairment in manic patients than in depressive patients. In this study, depressive patients with psychotic symptoms had poorer insight than those without psychosis, and manic patients had poor insight irrespective of the presence of psychotic symptoms.

Significant lack of insight on the social consequences of the illness in patients with psychotic mania has been also reported and it was inversely related to awareness of hallucination and delusion and their attributions (Dell'Osso et al. 2002; Pini et al. 2004). Yen et al. (2007) reported different lack of insight rates between psychotic bipolar cases at recovery period (36.36%) and non psychotic bipolar patients (9.37%), supporting that psychotic symptoms, especially delusions, rather than the severity of mania, is related to lack of insight.

3.10. Brain Structural Changes

Neuroanatomical basis of BD is complex and difficult to summary, due to the proliferation of methods and discrepant findings. A recent consensus functional neuroanatomic model has been proposed. In this model, disruption in early development (e.g., white matter connectivity and prefrontal pruning) within brain networks that modulate emotional behavior leads to decreased connectivity among ventral prefrontal networks and limbic brain regions, especially the amígdala (Strakowski et al, 2012). This would explain some of the reported anatomical abnormalities in BD: increased rates of hyperintense white matter lesions in subcortical and periventricular regions - the most consistently finding- (Bearden et al., 2001); reduced white matter volume in frontal regions (Kieseppa et al, 2003); reduced white matter volume in the frontal and temporo-parietal territory and in the corpus callosum (McDonald et al, 2005); global and prefrontal volumetric brain reductions, enlarged lateral ventricles and globus pallidus (Arnone et al, 2009). Specifically in regard to bipolar depression, neuropsychological and biochemical studies have found greater brain abnormalities (cognitive dysfunction related to frontal lobe hypoactivity and even reduction of its volume, subcortical hyper intensities on MRI, decreased N-acetylaspartate in dorsolateral prefrontal area) compared with unipolar depression, which may explain its association with more severe symptoms (Borkowska and Rybakowski, 2001; Ketter et al., 2004).

Bipolar patients have smaller lateral ventricular volume and enlarged amygdala volume comparing schizophrenic patients. Watson et al. (2012) investigated gray and white matter volume changes at first psychotic episode using voxel-based morphometry techniques in schizophrenic and bipolar patients. Their findings were: volume increase in the left tonsil region of the cerebellum; gray matter (GM) volume reduction in the right precuneus; white matter (WM) losses in the left superior frontal gyrus, in the inferior parietal lobe and in the tonsil region of the cerebellum and in the right cuneus. It also suggests white matter volume reduction in the right thalamus and right posterior cerebellum and bilateral GM volume increase in the cerebellar vermis region which in conflict with other studies that found cerebellum atrophy (Beyer at el., 2002; Brambilla et al., 2005). The study concluded that structural changes at first episode are much less prominent than in chronic illness.

The question if there is a potential neuroanatomical basis of the development of psychotic symptoms in BD has not yet accurately answered. One study observed more premorbid, morphological and neurocognitive changes in patients with psychotic symptoms (Mazziade et al, 1995). An explanation for this association would be that psychotic symptoms are a source of confusion in diagnosis and treatment, with a longer period of affective symptoms untreated and worse outcomes. Other study noted abnormalities of cerebral asymmetry in the postcentral gyrus of individuals with psychotic bipolar disorder, not present in those without psychotic symptoms (Reite et al, 1999). Another study found higher caudate dopamine D2-receptor density in bipolar patients with psychotic symptoms, similar to that found in schizophrenics (Pearlson et al, 1995). Finally, some researches (Velakoulis et al, 1999) have found reduced the left hippocampal volume or the left posterior amygdala-hippocampal complex (Hirayasu et al, 1998) in bipolar patients with psychotic features and schizophrenic patients.

3.11. Mixed States

Kraepelin already described relevance dimensions in mixed mania: mood -ranging from expansive to depressive-, psychomotor activity -excitability and inhibition- and speech or thought fluency. They described different mixed state subtypes: mania with anxiety and depressive symptoms; mania with anxiety and blunted speech; inhibited mania; stuporous mania; depression with accelerated speech; and agitated depression, which have been validated by other investigators (Akiskal et al., 2003; Perugi et al., 1997). Perugi et al. (2001) conducted a clinical characterization of depressive mixed state in patients with bipolar I disorder with a study that included 195 patients. Although they found similarities between the clinical and sociodemographic characteristics of the three groups studied (bipolar major depression, mixed state, depressive mixed state), it was found that non-congruouent psychotic features were more common in the two mixed groups compared to bipolar major depression, and the most common features of the depressive mixed state were agitation, psychotic depression with irritable mood, pressured speech and flight of ideas (Perugi et al., 2001). In the same line, Azorin et al. (2012) have studied the clinical heterogeneity of mixed states. Mixed states with predominant depressive symptoms showed more psychotic features, atypical features and suicide attempts during the index episode. Psychotic features and suicide attempts might be responsible for a greater severity of the depressive picture, leading to more frequent hospitalizations (Azorin et al., 2012).

More recently, the existence of excitatory features during major depression has been reported as the more prevalent subtype of bipolar mixed states (Akiskal and Benazzi, 2003; Sato et al., 2003). Winokur et al. (1985) found that patients with psychosis were more likely to have had no prior mood episodes and tearfulness as a symptom, suggesting that bipolar patients with psychosis were more likely to have mixed episodes than those without.

3.12. Cognitive Impairment

Nowadays, it is accepted the presence of some cognitive impairment in bipolar patients, although not so prominent as in schizophrenia. There is cognitive impairment beyond the acute manic and depressive episodes. Euthymic bipolar patients have attention and concentration failures, declarative memory and executive functions (Martinez Aran et al, 2001). This deficit has been associated with the number of episodes, subclinical psychopathology, negative symptoms, pharmacological treatment, functional outcome and psychotic symptoms (Strakowski et al., 2000; Tohen et al. 1992). Liu et al (2002) compared sustained attention deficits measured by the Continuous Performance Test in patients with various affective disorders and patients with schizophrenia. Patients with schizophrenia showed the most severe deficits, followed by the psychotic bipolar and finally the nonpsychotic bipolar patients. Authors suggest that attention deficit is a vulnerability marker for bipolar disorder that is shared with other individuals at high risk of psychotic spectrum disorders. However, the attention deficit in schizophrenia is not associated with the development of psychotic symptoms but, to a greater extent, it is related to the negative symptoms (Liu et al, 1996), formal thought disorder and disorganization (Pandurangi, 1994). Glahn et al (2007) observed that patients with bipolar disorder with previous history of psychosis were more impaired on executive functioning and have spatial working memory deficits compared with bipolar patients without history of psychosis.

One relevant study for our purpose (Martínez-Arán et al, 2008) addressed the specific question of a potential association between history of psychotic symptoms and a more pronounced cognitive deficit. Sixty-five euthymic bipolar disorder patients (35 with a history of psychotic symptoms and 30 without such a history) were assessed through a complete neuropsychological battery. Bipolar patients with a history of psychotic symptoms performed more poorly in all verbal memory measures and in tasks related to executive functions. Glahn et al (2007) investigated neurocognitive impairment in 69 bipolar I outpatients, considering presence or not of psychotic features, in comparison with a group of 35 healthy subjects. Overall, in bipolar I disorder, despite preserved general intellectual function, patients showed moderate impairments on episodic memory, psychomotor speed and attention. Nevertheless, psychotic bipolar disorder was associated with differential impairment on tasks requiring frontal/executive processing, suggesting that lifetime psychotic features may have neural correlates that are partially independent of those associated with bipolar I disorder more generally (Glahn et al., 2007). Likewise Tabarés-Seisdedos et al. (2003) found that patients with schizophrenia and those with bipolar I disorder with a positive family history of psychotic illness, performed significantly worse on tests of selective attention and visual–motor processing than patients without such a history (Tabarés-Seisdedos et al., 2003)

Given these evidences it is reasonable to hypothesize that bipolar patients with history of psychotic episodes, regarding the neuropsychological profile, are more similar to patients with primary psychosis –such as schizophrenia or schizoaffective disorder- than bipolar patients without history of psychotic features (Martinez-Aran et al., 2008)

3.13. Social Adjustment

Through long-term follow-up studies, Rosen et al. (1983a) and Tohen et al. (1990) reported that psychotic features in BD are predictive of worse psychosocial outcome. In a sample of 219 first affective episode with psychotic symptoms, 83,7 % showed symptomatic remission but only one third functional recovery. This result remarks the severe psychosocial impact of the irruption of psychotic symptoms for the bipolar patient. This effect is even more pronounced when psychotic symptoms are presented chronically (Coryell et al, 2001). Some studies have found that bipolar patients with mood-incongruent psychotic features had significantly worse psychosocial outcome and poorer social adjustment than bipolar patients with mood-congruent psychosis (Brockington et al, 1983; De Leon et al. 2000; Miklowitz 1992).

3.14. Comorbidity

Fifty per cent of first psychotic manic episodes presented any comorbidity, being substance abuse the most common (Strakowski et al, 1995). Tohen et al. (1998) found higher rates of personality disorders, substance abuse and anxiety disorders in the subgroup of psychotic mania. In a group of patients who were younger, with more paranoid ideas and worse prognosis, Carlson et al. (2000) found higher comorbidity of substance abuse and a history of behavior problems in childhood.

In conclusion, there are controversial results regarding the association between the development of psychotic symptoms in BD and other clinical and sociodemographic factors. With the above, we can classify the available scientific evidence on this association as follows:

- High level of evidence, with some controversy: family history of psychosis (regardless diagnostic categories); poor outcome and prognosis; and social disadjustment.
- Medium level of evidence, with high controversy: severity of manic symptoms; early age at onset; Afro-American race; lack of insight; specific brain abnormalities; mixed states; comorbidity; and cognitive impaiment.
- Low level or no evidence: personality; gender; and suicide risk.

References

Abrams R, Taylor MA. Catatonia: A prospective study. *Arch Gen Psychiatry* 1976; 33:579-81.

Abrams R, Taylor MA. Importance of schizophrenic symptoms in the diagnosis of mania. *Am J Psychiatry* 1981;138: 658-661.

Adebimpe VR, Chu CC, Klein HE, Lange MH. Racial and geographic differences in the psychopathology *Am J Psychiatry*. 1982 Jul;139(7):888-91.

Akiskal HS, Hantouche EG, Allilaire JF, Sechter D, Bourgeois ML, Azorin JM, Chatenêt-Duchêne L, Lancrenon S. Validating antidepressant *J Affect Disord.* 2003 Jan; 73(1-2): 65-74.

Akiskal HS, Benazzi F. Family history *J Affect Disord.* 2003 Jan; 73(1-2):113-22.

Akiskal HS, Puzantian VR. Psychotic forms of depression and mania. *Psychiatr Clin North Am* 1979; 2: 419-439.

Albus M, Hubmann W, Wahlheim C, Sobizack N, Franz U, Mohr F. Contrasts in neuropsychological test profile between patients with first-episode schizophrenia *Acta Psychiatr Scand.* 1996 Aug; 94(2):87-93.

Amador XF, Strauss DH, Yale SA, Flaum MM, Endicott J, Gorman JM. Assessment of insight in psychosis. *Am J Psychiatry.* 1993 Jun;150(6):873-9

American Psychiatric Association. *Diagnostic and Statistical Manual of Mental Disorders, 4th Edition,* Text Revision. Washington, DC. 2000.

American Psychiatric Association. Practice guideline for the treatment of patients with bipolar disorder (revision). *American Journal of Psychiatry* 2002;159:1–50.

Andreasen N. Thought, language and communication disorders: Diagnostic significance. *Arch. Gen. Psychiatry* 1979; 36, 1325–1330.

Andreasen NC, Rice J, Endicott J, Coryell W, Grove WM, Reich T. Familial rates of affective disorder. A report from the National Institute of Mental Health Collaborative Study. *Arch Gen Psychiatry.* 1987 May;44(5):461-9.

Angst J, Gamma A, Benazzi F, et al. Atypical depressive syndromes in varying definitions. *Eur Arch Psychiatry C!in Neurosci.* 2006;256:44-54.

Arnone D, Cavanagh J, Gerber D et al. Magnetic resonance imaging studies in bipolar disorder and schizophrenia: meta-analysis. *Br J Psychiatry.* 2009 Sep;195(3):194-201.

Austin MP: Puerperal affective psychosis: is there a case for lithium prophylaxis? *Br J Psychiatry* 1992, 161:692–694.

Axelsson R, Lagerkvist-Briggs M. Factors predicting suicide in psychotic patients. *Eur Arch Psychiatry Clin Neurosci.* 1992;241(5):259–66.

Azorin J-M, Akiskal H, Akiskal K, et al. Is psychosis in DSM-IV mania due to severity? The relevance of selected demographic and comorbid social-phobic features. *Acta Psychiatr Scand* 2007: 115: 29–34.

Azorin JM, Kaladjian A, Adida M et al. Risk factors associated with lifetime suicide attempts in bipolar I patients: findings from a French National Cohort. *Compr Psychiatry* 2009; 50: 115–120.

Azorin JM, Kaladjian A, Adida M, Fakra E, Belzeaux R, Hantouche E, Lancrenon S. Self-assessment and characteristics of mixed depression in the French national EPIDEP study. *J Affect Disord.* 2012 Dec;143(1-3):109-17.

Baethge C, Baldessarini RJ, Freudenthal K, Streeruwitz A, Bauer M, Bschor T. Hallucinations in bipolar disorder: characteristics and comparison to unipolar depression and schizophrenia. *Bipolar Disord.* 2005;7:136–145.

Bearden CE, Hoffman KM, Cannon TD. The neuropsychology and neuroanatomy of bipolar affective disorder: a critical review. *Bipolar Disord.* 2001 Jun;3(3):106-50; discussion 151-3.

Beckmann H, Fritze J, Lanczik M: Prognostic validity of the cycloid psychoses. A prospective follow-up study. *Psychopathology* 1990, 23:205–211.

Beigel A, Murphy DL. Assesing clinical characteristics of the manic state. *Am J Psychiatry.* 1971;128:688-694.

Benazzi F. Bipolar versus unipolar psychotic outpatient depression. *J Affect Disord.* 1999a;55:63–66.

Benazzi F. Gender differences in bipolar II and unipolar depressed outpatients: A 557-case study. *Ann Clin Psychiatry.* 1999;11:55-59.

Benazzi F. Psychotic versus nonpsychotic bipolar outpatient depression. *Eur Psychiatry* 1999b;14:458-61.

Beyer JL, Krishnan KR. Volumetric brain imaging findings in mood disorders. *Bipolar Disord* 2002;4(2):89–104.

Black D, Winokur G, Nasrallah A. Effect of psychosis on suicide risk in 1,593 patients with unipolar and bipolar affective disorders. *Am J Psychiatry.* 1988;145(7):849–52.

Black DW, Nasrallah A. Hallucinations and delu- sions in 1715 patients with unipolar and bipolar affective disorders. *Psychopathology.* 1989;22:28-34.

Blacker D, Tsuang MT. Contested boundaries of bipolar disorder and the limits of categorical diagnosis in psychiatry. *Am J Psychiatry* 1992; 149: 1473-1483.

Blairy S, Massat I, Staner L, Le Bon O, Van Gestel S, Van Broeckhoven C, et al. 5HT2a receptor polymorphism gene in bipolar disorder and harm avoidance personality trait. *American Journal of Medical Genetics* 2000;96:360–364.

Bleuler Eugen:"Dementia Praecox oder Gruppe der Schizophrenien", Traité d'Aschaffenburg, 1911. *Traducción española: Demencia precoz o el grupo de las esquizofrenias.* Buenos Aires: Hormé, 1993.

Borkowska A, Rybakowski JK. Neuropsychological frontal lobe tests indicate that bipolar depressed patients are more impaired than unipolar. *Bipolar Disord.* 2001;3:88–94.

Brambilla P, Glahn DC, Balestrieri M, Soares JC. Magnetic resonance findings in bipolar disorder. *Psychiatr Clin N Am* 2005;28(2):443–67.

Bräunig P, Krüger S, Shugar G. Prevalence and clinical significance of catatonic symptoms in mania. *Compr Psychiatry.* 1998 Jan-Feb;39(1):35-46.

Braunig P, Sarkar R, Effenberger S, et al. *Gender Differences in Psychotic Bipolar Mania Gender Medicine/*Vol 6, No.2, 2009.

Brockington IF, Hillier VF, Francis AF, Helzer JE, Wainwright S. Definitions of mania: concordance and predictions of outcome. *Am J Psychiatr* 1983; 140: 435-439

Brugue E, Colom F, Sanchez-Moreno J, Cruz N, Vieta E. Depression Subtypes in Bipolar I and II Disorders. *Psychopathology.* 2008;41:111–114.

Caetano SC, Olvera RL, Hunter K, Hatch JP, Najt P, Bowden C, Pliszka S, Soares JC. Association of psychosis with suicidality in pediatric bipolar I, II and bipolar NOS patients. *J Affect Disord.* 2006;91:33-37.

Canuso CM, Bossie CA, Zhu Y, et al. Psychotic symptoms in patients with bipolar mania. *Journal of Affective Disorders* 111, 2008; 164–169.

Cardno AG, Rijsdijk FV, Sham PC, Murray RM, McGuffin P. A twin study of genetic relationships between psychotic symptoms. *Am J Psychiatry.* 2002;159(4):539–545.

Carlson GA, Bromet EJ, Sievers S: Phenomenology and outcome of subjects with early- and adult-onset psychotic mania. *Am J Psychiatry* 2000; 157:213–219

Carlson GA, Goodwin FK: The stages of mania. A longitudinal analysis of the manic episode. *Arch Gen Psychiatry* 1973, 28:221–228.

Carlson GA, Strober M. Affective disorders in adolescence. *Psychiatr Clin North Am* 1979; 2:511–526.

Cloninger CR, Bayon C, Svrakic DM. Measurement of temperament and carácter in mood disorders: a modelo f fundamental states as personality types. *Journal of Affective Disorders* 1998; 51: 21-32.

Cohen LS, Sichel DA, Robertson LM, et al.: Postpartum prophylaxis for women with bipolar disorder. *Am J Psychiatry* 1995, 52:1641–1645.

Coryell W, Keller M, Lavori P (1990) Affective syndromes, psychotic features, and prognosis, II: mania. *Arch Gen Psychiatry* 47:658–664.

Copeland LA, Zeber JE, Salloum IM, Pincus HA, Fine MJ, Kilbourne AM. Treatment adherence and illness insight in veterans with bipolar disorder *J Nerv Ment Dis*. 2008 Jan; 196(1):16-21.

Coryell W, Leon AC, Turvey C, et al. The significance of psychotic features in manic episodes: a report from the NIMH collaborative study. *Journal of Affective Disorders* 67 (2001) 79–88.

Cutting J: Relationship between cycloid psychosis and typical affective psychosis. *Psychopathology* 1990, 23:212–219.

David AS. Insight and psychosis. *Br J Psychiatry*. 1990 Jun;156:798-808

Debowska G, Grzywa A, Kucharska-Pietura K. Insight in paranoid schizophrenia—its relationship to psychopathology and premorbid adjustment. *Compr Psychiatry*. 1998; 39(5):255-60.

De Leon J, Gonzalez-Pinto A, Mosquera F, Guiterrez M, De Heredia JLP, Excurra J. *Psychosis and bipolar disorder*. New Research Abstracts of the American Psychiatric Association Annual Meeting, Chicago, IL, May 2000 (abstr 431).

Dell'Osso L, Pini S, Cassano GB et al. (2002) Insight into illness in patients with mania, mixed mania, bipolar depression and major depression with psychotic features. *Bipolar Disord*, 4: 315–322.

Dell'Osso L, Pini S, Tundo A et al. (2000) Clinical characteristics of mania,mixed mania and bipolar depression with psychotic features. *Compr Psychiatry,* 41: 242–247.

Dickerson FB, Boronow JJ, Ringel N, Parente F. Lack of insight among outpatients with schizophrenia. *Psychiatric Services* (Washington, D.C.) 1997; 48(2): 195-9.

Dunayevich, E., Keck, P.E., 2000. Prevalence and description of psychotic features in bipolar mania. *Curr. Psychiatry Rep*. 2, 286–290.

Earle-Boyer EA, Levinson JC, Grant R, Harvey PD: The consistency of thought disorder in mania and schizophrenia. II. An assessment at consecutive admissions. *J Nerv Ment Dis* 1986, 174:443–447.

Engstrom C, Brandstrom S, Sigvardsson S, Cloninger CR, Nylander PO. Bipolar disorder. II: Personality and age of onset. *Bipolar Disorders* 2003;5:340–348.

Engstrom C, Brandstrom S, Sigvardsson S, Cloninger CR, Nylander PO. Bipolar disorder I. Temperament and character. *Journal of Affective Disorders* 2004a;82:131–134.

Engstrom C, Brandstrom S, Sigvardsson S, Cloninger CR, Nylander PO. Bipolar disorder. III: Harm avoidance a risk factor for suicide attempts. *Bipolar Disorders* 2004b;6:130–138.

Evans L, Akiskal HS, Keck PE Jr, McElroy SL, Sadovnick AD, Remick RA, et al. Familiality of temperament in bipolar disorder: support for a genetic spectrum. *Journal of Affective Disorders* 2005;85:153–168.

Fennig S, Bromet EJ, Karant MT, et al.: Mood-congruent versus mood-incongruent psychotic symptoms in first-admission patients with affective disorder. *J Affect Disord* 1996, 37:23–29.

Finseth PI, Morken G, Andreassen OA, Malt UF, Vaaler AE. Risk factors related to lifetime suicide attempts in acutely admitted bipolar disorder inpatients. *Bipolar Disord* 2012: 14: 727–734.

Gaudiano BA, Uebelacker LA, Miller IW. Course of Illness in Psychotic Mania: Is Mood Incongruence Important?. *J Nerv Ment Dis* 2007;195: 226–232.

Geller B, Tillman R, Craney JL, Bolhofner K. Four-year prospective outcome and natural history *Arch Gen Psychiatry*. 2004 May; 61(5):459-67.

Ghaemi SN, Rosenquist KJ. Is insight in mania *J Nerv Ment Dis*. 2004 Nov; 192(11):771-5

Glahn DC, Bearden CE, Barguil M, Barrett J, Reichenberg A, Bowden CL, Soares JC, Velligan DI. The neurocognitive signature of psychotic bipolar disorder. *Biol. Psychiatry*. 2007;62:910–916.

Goes FS, Sadler B, Toolan J, Zamoiski RD, Mondimore FM, MacKinnon DF, Schweizer B, DePaulo Jr JR, Potash JB. Psychotic features in bipolar and unipolar depression. *Bipolar Disord*. 2007;9:901–906.

Goldberg JF, Harrow M, Grossman LS. Course and outcome in bipolar affective disorder: a longitudinal follow-up study. Am J Psychiatry 1995;152:379-384.

Goldberg JF, Harrow M. Consistency of remission and outcome in bipolar and unipolar mood disorders: a 10-year prospective follow-up. *J Affect Disord*. 2004;81(2):123–131.

Goldstein TR, Birmaher B, Axelson D, et al. History of suicide attempts in pediatric bipolar disorder: factors associated with increased risk. *Bipolar Disord* 2005: 7: 525–535.

Gonzalez JM, Bowden CL, Berman N et al., One-Year Treatment Outcomes of African-American and Hispanic Patients With Bipolar I or II Disorder in STEP-BD. *Psychiatric Services* (Washington, D.C.). 2010 Feb; 61(2)164-172

Gonzalez-Pinto A, Gutierrez M, Mosquera F, Ballesteros J, Lopez P, Ezcurra J, Figuerido JL, de Leon J. First episode in bipolar disorder: misdiagnosis and psychotic symptoms. *J Affect Disord*. 1998 Jul;50(1):41-4.

González-Pinto A, Reed C, Novick D, Bertsch J, Haro JM. Assessment of medication adherence in a cohort of patients with bipolar disorder. *Pharmacopsychiatry*. 2010 Nov;43(7):263-70.

Goodwin DW, Alderson P, Rosenthal R. Clinical significance of hallucinations in psychiatric disorders. A study of 116 hallucinatory patients. *Arch Gen Psychiatry*. 1971 Jan;24(1):76-80.

Goodwin, F.K., Jamison, K.R., 1990. *Manic–Depressive Illness*. Oxford University Press, New York, NY.

Goodwin FK, Redfield Jamison K.*Manic-Depressive Illness: Bipolar Disorders and Recurrent Depression. 2nd ed.* New York, NY: Oxford University Press; 2007.

Goodwin GM, Anderson I, Arango C, Bowdend CL, Henry C, Mitchell PB, Nolen WA, Vieta E, Wittchen HU. ECNP consensus meeting. Bipolar depression. Nice, March 2007. *Eur Neuropsychopharmacol*. 2008;18:535–549.

Grunebaum MF, Oquendo MA, Harkavy-Friedman JM et al. Delusions and suicidality. *Am J Psychiatry* 2001; 158: 742–747.

Grunze H, Vieta E, Goodwin GM, Bowden C, Licht RW, Möller HJ, Kasper S; WFSBP Task Force On Treatment Guidelines For Bipolar Disorders. The world federation of societies of biological psychiatry (WFSBP) guidelines for the biological treatment of bipolar disorders: update 2010 on the treatment of acute bipolar depression. *World J Biol Psychiatry*. 2010 Mar;11(2):81-109.

Güçlü O, Karaca O, Yıldırım B, Ozköse MM, Erkıran M. The relationship between insight and clinical features in bipolar disorder. *Turk Psikiyatri Derg*. 2011; 22(4): 230-8.

Haro, J.M, van Os, J, Vieta, E, et al. Evidence for three distinct classes of 'typical', 'psychotic' and 'dual' mania: results from the EMBLEM study. *Acta Psychiatr. Scand*. 2006 Feb; 113(2): 112–120.

Harrow M, Goldberg JF, Grossman LS, Meltzer HY. Outcome in manic *Arch Gen Psychiatry*. 1990 Jul; 47(7):665-71.

Helzer JE. Bipolar affective disorder in black and white men. A comparison of symptoms and familial illness. *Arch Gen Psychiatry*. 1975; 32(9):1140-3.

Hendrick V, Altshuler LL, Gitlin MJ, Delrahim S, Hammen C. Gender and bipolar illness *J Clin Psychiatry*. 2000 May;61(5):393-6; quiz 397.

Hirayasu Y, Shenton ME, Salisbury DF, Dickey CC, Fischer IA, Mazzoni P, P, Kisler T, Arakaki H, Kwon JS, Anderson JE, Yurgelun-Todd D, Tohen M, McCarley RW. Lower left temporal lobe MRI volumes in patients with first-episode schizophrenia compared with psychotic patients with first-episode affective disorder and normal subjects. *Am J Psychiatry*. 1998 Oct;155(10):1384-91.

Hu C, Xiang YT, Ungvari GS, Dickerson FB, Kilbourne AM, Si TM, Fang YR, Lu Z, Yang HC, Chiu HF, Lai KY, Hu J, Chen ZY, Huang Y, Sun J, Wang XP, Li HC, Zhang JB, Wang G. Undiagnosed bipolar disorder in patients treated for major depression in China. *J Affect Disord*. 2012;140:181–186.

Hua LL, Wilens TE, Martelon M, et al. Psychosocial functioning, familiality, and psychiatric comorbidity in bipolar youth with and without psychotic features. *J Clin Psychiatry*. 2011 Mar;72(3):397-405.

Ivleva E, Thaker G, Tamminga C. Comparing Genes and Phenomenology in the Major Psychoses: Schizophrenia and Bipolar 1 Disorder. *Schizophrenia Bulletin*. 2008;34(4):734–742.

Jampala VC, Taylor MA, Abrams R: The diagnostic implications of formal thought disorder in mania and schizophrenia: a reassessment. *Am J Psychiatry* 1989, 146:459–463.

Jaspers K. Allgemeine Psychopathologie. Springer Verlag, Berlin, 1913; Traducción: Jaspers K. *Psicopatología General. México, Fondo de Cultura Económica*, 1996.

Johnson SL, McMurrich SL, Yates M (2005) Suicidality in bipolar I disorder. *Suicide Life Threat Behav*. 35: 681–689.

Judd LL, Akiskal HS, Schettler PJ, Endicott J, Maser J, Solomon DA, Leon AC, Rice JA, Keller MB. The long-term natural history *Arch Gen Psychiatry*. 2002 Jun; 59(6):530-7.

Kay, S.R., Opler, L.A., Fiszbein, A., 2000. *Positive and Negative Syndrome Scale User's Manual*. Multi-Health Systems Inc., North Tonawanda, NY.

Keck Jr PE, McElroy SL, Havens JR, Altshuler LL, Nolen WA, Frye MA, Suppes T, Denicoff KD, Kupka R, Leverich GS, Rush AJ, Post RM. Psychosis in bipolar disorder: phenomenology and impact on morbidity and course of illness. *Compr. Psychiatry*. 2003;44:263–269.

Kendler KS. Mood-incongruent psychotic affective ill- ness. *Arch Gen Psychiatry* 1991;48:362-369.

Kendler KS, McGuire M, Gruenberg AM, O'Hare A, Spellman M, Walsh D. The Roscommon family study. III. Schizophrenia-related personality disorders in relatives. *Arch Gen Psychiatry* 1993;50: 781–8.

Kennedy N, Boydell J, van Os J, Murray RM. Ethnic differences in first clinical presentation of bipolar disorder: Results from an epidemiological study. *J Affect Disord* 2004; 83:161–168.

Kessing LV. Subtypes of manic *J Affect Disord*. 2004 Sep; 81(3):279-85.

Ketter TA, Wang PW, Becker OV, Nowakowska C, Yang YS. Psychotic bipolar disorders: dimensionally similar to or categorically different from schizophrenia? *Journal of Psychiatric Research.* 2004;38:47–61.

Kieseppä T, Van Erp TG, Haukka J, Partonen T, Cannon TD, Poutanen VP, Kaprio J, Lönnqvist J. Reduced left hemispheric white matter *Biol Psychiatry.* 2003 Nov 1; 54(9):896-905.

Kowatch RA, Youngstrom EA, Danielyan A, et al. Review and meta-analysis of the phenomenology and clinical characteristics of mania in children and adolescents. *Bipolar Disord.* 2005;7:483–496.

Kraepelin, E. In *Manic-Depressive Insanity and Paranoia.* New York: Arno Press; 1976. Fundamental States; p. 117-132.

Kufferle B, Lenz G, Schanda H: Clinical evaluation of language and thought disorders in patients with schizophrenic and affective psychoses. *Psychopathology* 1985, 18:126–132.

Lahera G., Montes JM., Benito A., Sáiz-Ruiz J. Associated factors to the development of psychotic symptoms in bipolar mania. *Archivos de Psiquiatría* 2006; Vol. 69, n. 2

Leadholm AK, Rothschild AJ, Nolen WA, Bech P, Munk-Jørgensen P, Ostergaard SD. The treatment of psychotic depression: Is there consensus among guidelines and psychiatrists? *J Affect Disord.* 2012 Sep 27. [Epub ahead of print].

Leonhard K. *Classification of endogenous psychosis and their differenciated etiology.* Ed 2nd, New York: Springer-Velag Wein, 1999.

Liu CY, Bai YM, Yang YY, Lin CC, Sim CC, Lee CH. Suicide and parasuicide in psychiatric inpatients: ten years experience at a general hospital in Taiwan *Psychol Rep.* 1996 Oct; 79(2):683-90.

Liu SK, Chiu CH, Chang CJ, Hwang TJ, Hwu HG, Chen WJ. Deficits in sustained attention in schizophrenia and affective disorders: stable versus state-dependent markers. *Am J Psychiatry* 2002; 159: 975 - 982

López-Larson MP, DelBello MP, Zimmerman ME, Schwiers ML, Strakowski SM. Regional prefrontal gray and white matter abnormalities in bipolar disorder. *Biol Psychiatry.* 2002 Jul 15;52(2):93-100.

López P, Mosquera F, de León J, Gutiérrez M, Ezcurra J, Ramírez F, González-Pinto A. Suicide attempts in bipolar patients. *J Clin Psychiatry.* 2001 Dec;62(12):963-6.

Lowe GR. The phenomenology of hallucinations as an aid to differential diagnosis. *Br J Psychiatry.* 1973 Dec; 123 (577):621-33.

Lundquist G. Prognosis and course in manic-depressive psychoses. A follow-up study of 319 first admissions. *Acta Psychiatr Neurol* 1945;35(Suppl):5-93.

Maier W, Lichtermann D, Minges J, Heun R, Hallmayer J, Benkert O. Schizoaffective disorder and affective disorders with mood-incongruent psychotic features: keep separate or combine? Evidence from a family study. *Am J Psychiatry*. 1992 Dec;149(12):1666-73.

Maj M: Cycloid psychotic disorder: validation of the concept by means of a follow-up and a family study. *Psychopathology* 1990, 23:196–204.

Mantere O, Isometsa E, Ketokivi M et al. A prospective latent analyses study of psychiatric comorbidity of DSM-IV bipolar I and II disorders. *Bipolar Disord* 2010: 12: 271–284.

Mantere O, Suominen K, Leppamaki S, Valtonen H, Arvilommi P, Isometsa E. The clinical characteristics of DSM-IV bipolar I and II disorders: baseline findings from the Jorvi Bipolar Study (JoBS). *Bipolar Disord.* 2004;6:395–405.

Martinez-Aran A, Torrent C, Tabares-Seisdedos R, Salamelo M, Daban C, Balanza-Martinez V, Sanchez-Moreno J, Goikolea J, Benabarre A, Colom F, Vieta E. Neurocognitive impairment in bipolar patients with and without history of psychosis. *J. Clin. Psychiatry*. 2008;69:233–239.

Martínez-Arán, A. Deterioro cognitivo y trastorno bipolar. *I Congreso Virtual de Psiquiatría 1 de Febrero - 15 de Marzo 2000* (citado 17 de Agosto 2006); Conferencia 31-CI-A.

Martínez-Arán A, Goodwin GM, Vieta E. El mito de la ausencia de disfunciones cognitivas en el trastorno bipolar. En: *Trastornos Bipolares. Avances clínicos y terapéuticos*. Ed Panamericana, Madrid, 2001.

Mazzarini L, Colom F, Pacchiarotti I, Nivoli AM, Murru A, Bonnin CM, Cruz N, Sanchez-Moreno J, Kotzalidis GD, Girardi P, et al. Psychotic versus non-psychotic bipolar II disorder. *J Affect Disord*. 2010;126(1-2):55-60.

Mazziade M, Roy MA, Martínez M et al. Negative psychoticism and disorganized dimensions in patients with familial schizophrenia or bipolar disorder: continuity and discontinuity between the major psychosis. *Am J Psychiatry* 1995; 152: 1348 – 1363.

McDonald C, Bullmore E, Sham P, et al. Regional volume deviations of brain structure in schizophrenia and psychotic bipolar disorder: computational morphometry study. *Br J Psychiatry*. 2005 May;186:369-77.

McElroy SL, Altshuler LL, Suppes T, Keck PE et al. Axis I Psychiatric Comorbidity and its relationship to historical illness variables in 288 patients with bipolar disorder. *Am J Psychiatry* 2001; 158, 3.

McElroy SL, Keck PE Jr, Strakowski SM: Mania, psicosis and antipsychotics. *J Clin Psychiatry* 1996, 57(Suppl 3):14–26.

McElroy SL, Strakowski SM, West SA, Keck PE, McConville BJ. Phenomenology of adolescent and adult mania in hospitalised patients with Bipolar Disorder. *Am J Psychiatry* 1997; 154:44–49.

McGlashan TH. Adolescent versus adult onset of mania. *Am J Psychiatry* 1988. 145:221–223.

Mendlewicz J, Fieve RR, Stallone F, Fleiss JL. Genetic history as a predictor of lithium response in manic-depressive illness. *Lancet.* 1972 Mar 11;1(7750):599-600.

Michalakeas A, Skoutas C, Charalambous A, Peristeris A, Marinos V, Keramari E, Theologou A. Insight in schizophrenia and mood disorders and its relation to psychopathology. *Acta Psychiatr Scand.* 1994; 90: 46 – 49.

Miklowitz DJ, Goldstein MJ, Nuechterlein KH, Snyder KS, Mintz J. Family factors and the course of bipolar affective disorder. *Arch Gen Psychiatry* 1988; 45: 225-231

Miklowitz DJ. Longitudinal outcome and medication noncompliance among manic patients with and without mood-incongruent psychotic features. *J nerv Ment Dis* 1992; 180: 703-711

Minsky S, Vega W, Miskimen T, Gara M, Escobar J. Diagnostic patterns in Latino, African American and European American psychiatric patients. *Arch Gen Psychiatry* 2003; 60:637–644.

Mitchell PB, Goodwin GM, Johnson GF, Hirschfeld RMA. Diagnostic guidelines for bipolar depression: a probabilistic approach. *Bipolar Disord.* 2008;10:144–152.

Mitchell PB, Malhi GS. Bipolar depression: phenomenological overview and clinical characteristics. *Bipolar Disord.* 2004;6:530–539.

Murphy DL, Beigel A. Depression, elation, and lithium *Arch Gen Psychiatry.* 1974 Nov; 31(5):643-8.

Oquendo MA, Waternaux C, Brodsky B, Parsons B, Haas GL, Malone KM, Mann JJ. Suicidal behavior in bipolar mood disorder: Clinical characteristics of attempters and nonattempters. *J Affect Disord.* 2000;59:107-117.

Oosthuizen P, Russouw H, Roberts M. Is puerperal psychosis bipolar mood disorder?: a phenomenological comparison. *Compr Psychiatry.* 1995 Jan-Feb;36(1):77-81.

Osher Y, Cloninger CR, Belmaker RH. TPQ in euthymic manic-depressive patients. *Journal of Psychiatric Research* 1996;30:353–357.

Osher Y, Lefkifker E, Kotler M. Low persistence in euthymic manic-depressive patients: a replication. *Journal of Affective Disorders* 1999;53:87–90.

Ostergaard SD, Bertelsen A, Nielsen J, Mors O, Petrides G. The association between psychotic mania *J Affect Disord.* 2012 Oct 30.

Pandurangi AK, Sax KW, Pelonero AL, Goldberg SC. Sustained attention and positive formal disorder in schizophrenia. Schizophr Res 1994; 13: 109 – 116.

Papolos D, Hennen J, Cockerham MS (2005) Factors associated with parent-reported suicide threats by children and adolescents with community-diagnosed bipolar disorder. *J Affect Disord.* 86: 267–275.

Parker G, Roy K, Wilhelm K, Mitchell P, Hadzi-Pavlovic, D. The nature of bipolar depression: implications for the definition of melancholia. *J Affect Disord.* 2000;59:217–224.

Pavuluri MN, Birmaher B, Naylor M. Pediatric bipolar disorder: A review of the past 10 years. *J Am Acad Child Adolesc Psychiatry.* 2005;44(9):846–71.

Pearlson GD, Wong DF, Tune LE, et al. In vivo D2 dopamine receptor density in psychotic and nonpsychotic patients with bipolar disorder. *Arch Gen Psychiatry* 1995; 52: 471 – 477.

Pease E. A note on the prognostic value of hallucinations in the manic-depressive psicosis. *Am J Insanity.* 1912; 69: 1-36.

Peralta V, Cuesta MJ. Lack of insight in mood disorders. *J Affect Disord* 1998; 46:55-58.

Perlis RH, Brown E, Baker R, Nierenberg A. Clinical Features of Bipolar Depression versus Major Depressive Disorder in Large Multicenter Trials. *Am J Psychiatry.* 2006;163:225-231.

Perron BE, Fries LE, Kilbourne AM et al. Racial/Ethnic Group Differences in Bipolar Symptomatology in a Community Sample of Persons With Bipolar I Disorder. *J Nerv Ment Dis* 2010;198: 16–21.

Perugi G, Akiskal HS, Micheli C, Toni C, Madaro D. Clinical characterization of depressive mixed state in bipolar-I patients: Pisa–San Diego collaboration. *J Affect Disord.* 2001;67:105–114.

Perugi G, Micheli C, Akiskal HS, Madaro D, Socci C, Quilici C, Musetti L. Polarity of the first episode, clinical characteristics, and course of manic depressive illness: a systematic retrospective in- vestigation of 320 bipolar I patients. *Compr Psychiatry* 2000; 41:13–18.

Perugi G, Akiskal HS, Micheli C, Musetti L, Paiano A, Quilici C, Rossi L, Cassano GB. Clinical subtypes of bipolar mixed states *J Affect Disord.* 1997 May;43(3):169-80.

Perugi G, Akiskal HS, Rossi L, Paiano A, Quilici C, Madaro D, Musetti L, Cassano GB. Chronic mania: family history, prior course, clinical picture and social consequences. *Br J Psychiatry* 1999; 173: 514–518.

Petursson H: Lithium treatment of a patient with periodic catatonia. *Acta Psychiatr Scand* 1976, 54:248–253.

Pini S, de Queiroz V, Dell'Osso L, Abelli M, Mastrocinque C, Saettoni M, Catena M, Cassano GB. Cross-sectional similarities and differences between schizophrenia *Eur Psychiatry*. 2004 Feb; 19(1):8-14.

Pope HG Jr, Lipinski JF Jr. Diagnosis in schizophrenia and manic-depressive illness: A reassessment of the specificity of 'schizophrenic' symptoms in the light of current research. *Arch Gen Psychiatry*. 1978; 35: 811-828.

Potash JB, Willour VL, Chiu YF, et al. The familial aggregation of psychotic symptoms in bipolar disorder pedigrees. *Am J Psychiatry*. 2001 Aug;158(8):1258-64.

Potash JB, Zandi PP, Willour VL, Lan TH, Huo Y, Avramopoulos D, Shugart YY, MacKinnon DF, Simpson SG, McMahon FJ, DePaulo Jr JR, McInnis MG. Suggestive linkage to chromosomal regions 13q 31 and 22q12 in families with psychotic bipolar disorder. *Am. J. Psychiatry*. 2003;160:680–686.

Reite M, Teale P, Rojas DC, Arciniegas D, Sheeder J. Bipolar disorder: anomalous brain asymmetry associated with psychosis. *Am J Psychiatry*. 1999 Aug; 156(8):1159-63.

Rogers G, Joyce P, Mulder R, Sellman D, Miller A, Allington M, et al. Association of a duplicated repeat polymorphism in the 5'-untranslated region of the DRD4 gene with novelty seeking. *American Journal of Medical Genetics. Part B.* Neuropsychiatric Genetics: the official publication of the International Society of Psychiatric Genetics 2004;126:95–98.

Rosen LN, Rosenthal NE, Van Dusen PH, Dunner DL, Fieve RR. Age at onset and number of psychotic symptoms in bipolar I and schizoaffective disorder. *Am J Psychiatry* 1983; 140: 1523-1524.

Rosen NL, Rosenthal NE, Dunner DL, Fieve RR. Social outcome compared in psychotic and nonpsychotic bipolar I patients. *J Nerv Ment Dis* 1983 ; 171: 272-275.

Rosenthal D, Wender PH, Kety SS, Welner J, Schulsinger F.The adopted-away offspring of schizophrenics. *Am J Psychiatry*. 1971 Sep;128(3):307-11.

Rosenthal NE, Rosenthal LN, Stallone F, Dunner DL, Fleve RR. Toward the validation of RDC schizoaffective disorder. *Arch Gen Psychiatr* 1980; 37: 804-810.

Rosenthal NE, Rosenthal LN, Stallone F: Psychosis as a predictor of response to lithium maintenance treatment in bipolar affective disorder. *J Affect Disord* 1979; 1: 237-245.

Roy-Byrne P, Post RM, Uhde TW, et al. The longitudinal course of recurrent affective illness: Life chart data from research patients at the NIMH. *Acta Psychiatr Scand Suppl*. 1985;317:1-34.

Sachs GS, Printz DJ, Kahn DA, Carpenter D, Docherty JP. The Expert Consensus Guideline Series: Medication Treatment of Bipolar Disorders 2000. *Postgraduate Medicine Spec*. 2000:1–104.

Sato T, Bottlender R, Kleindienst N, Moller HJ. Syndromes and phenomenological subtypes underlying acute mania: a factor analytic study of 576 manic patients. *Am J Psychiatry* 2002;159:968–974.

Sato T, Bottlender R, Schröter A, Möller HJ. Frequency of manic *Acta Psychiatr Scand*. 2003 Apr; 107(4):268-74.

Sax KW, Strakowski SM, Keck PE, McElroy SL, West SA, Bourne ML, Larson ER. Comparison of patients with early-, typical-, and late-onset affective psychosis. *Am J Psychiatry* 1997; 154:1299–1301.

Schoptf J, Rust B. Follow up and family study of post partum psychosis. Part I: overview. *Eur Arch Psychiatry Clin Neurosci* 1994, 244: 101-111.

Simpson SG, Jamison KR. The risk of suicide in patients with bipolar disorders. *J Clin Psychiatry*. 1999;60 Suppl 2:53-6.

Slama F, Bellivier F, Henry C, Rousseva A, Etain B, Rouillon F, Leboyer M. Bipolar patients with suicidal behavior: toward the identification of a clinical subgroup. *J Clin Psychiatry*. 2004 Aug;65(8):1035-9.

Song JY, Yu HY, Kim SH, Hwang SS, Cho HS, Kim YS, Ha K, Ahn YM. Assessment of Risk Factors Related to Suicide Attempts in Patients With Bipolar Disorder. *J Nerv Ment Dis*. 2012;200:978-984.

Staner L, Hilger C, Hentges F, Monreal J, Hoffmann A, Couturier M. Association between novelty seeking and the dopamine D3 receptor gene in bipolar patients: a preliminary report. *American Journal of Medical Genetics* 1998;81:192–194.

Stewart DE, Klompenhouwer JL, Kendell RE, van Hulst AM: Prophylactic lithium in puerperal psychosis. The experience of three centres. *Br J Psychiatry* 1991, 158:393–397.

Strakowski SM, Adler CM, Almeida J, Altshuler LL, Blumberg HP, Chang KD, DelBello MP, Frangou S, McIntosh A, Phillips ML, Sussman JE, Townsend JD. The functional neuroanatomy of bipolar disorder: a consensus model. *Bipolar Disord.* 2012 Jun;14(4):313-25

Strakowski SM, Keck PE, McElroy SL et al. Chronology of comorbid and principal síndromes in first-episode psicosis. *Compr Psychiatry*, 1995; 6: 1-8

Strakowski SM, McElroy SL, Keck PE Jr, West SA. Racial influence on diagnosis in psychotic mania. *J Affect Disord.* 1996 Jul 8;39(2):157-62

Strakowski SM, Williams JR, Sax KW, Fleck DE, Del- Bello MP, Bourne ML. Is impaired outcome following a first manic episode due to mood-incongruent psychosis? *J Affect Disord* 2000;61:87-94.

Strober M, Lampert C, Schmidt S, Morrell W. The course of major depressive disorder in adolescents: 1. Recovery and risk of manic switching in a follow-up of psychotic and nonpsychotic subtypes. *J Am Acad Child Adolesc Psychiatry.* 1993;32:32–42.

Swann, A.C., Daniel, D.G., Kochan, L.D., Wozniak, P.J., Calabrese, J.R., 2004. Psychosis in mania: specificity of its role in severity and treatment response. *J. Clin. Psychiatry* 65, 825–829.

Swann AC, Janicak PL, Calabrese JR et al. Structure of mania: depressive, irritable, and psychotic clusters with different retrospectively-assessed course patterns of illness in randomized clinical trial participants. *J Affect Disord* 2001;67:123–132.

Tabarés-Seisdedos R, Balanzá-Martínez V, Salazar-Fraile J, Selva-Vera G, Leal-Cercós C, Gómez-Beneyto M. Specific executive/attentional deficits in patients with schizophrenia or bipolar disorder who have a positive family history of psychosis. *J. Psychol. Res.* 2003;37:479–486.

Taylor MA, Abrams R. Acute mania *Arch Gen Psychiatry.* 1975 Jul; 32(7): 863-5.

Tillman R, Geller B, Klages T, et al. Psychotic phenomena in 257 young children and adolescents with bipolar I disorder: delusions and hallucinations (benign and pathological). *Bipolar Disord* 2008: 10: 45–55.

Tohen M, Greenfield SF, Weiss RD et al. The effect of comorbid substance use disorders on the course of bipolar disorder: a review. *Harv Rev Psychiatry* 1998; 6: 133-141

Tohen M, Hennen J, Zarate C, Baldessarini RJ, Strakowski SM, Stoll A, Faeda GL, Suppes T, Gebre-Mehdin P, Cohen B. Two-year syndromal and functional recovery in 219 cases of first-episode major affective disorder with psychotic features. *Am J Psychiatry* 2000; 157: 220-228

Tohen M, Khalsa HM, Salvatore P, Vieta E, Ravichandran C, Baldessarini RJ. Two-year outcomes in first-episode psychotic depression the McLean-Harvard First-Episode Project. *J Affect Disord.* 2012 Jan;136(1-2):1-8.

Tohen M, Tsuang MT, Goodwin DC: Prediction of outcome in mania by mood-congruent or mood-incongruent psychotic features. *Am J Psychiatry* 1992, 149:1580–1584.

Tohen M, Waternaux CM, Tsuang MT. Outcome in mania: a 4-year prospective follow-up of 75 patients utilizing survival analysis. *Arch Gen Psychiatry* 1990; 47:1106–1111

Tohen M, Zarate CA, Hennen J et al. The McLean-Harvard First-Episode Mania Study: Prediction of Recovery and First Recurrence. *Am J Psychiatry* 2003;160:2099-2107.

Toni C, Perugi G, Mata B et al. Is mood-incongruent manic psychosis a distinct subtype? *Eur Arch Psychiatry Clin Neurosci* (2001) 251 : 12–17

Torrent C, Martinez-Arán A, del Mar Bonnin C, Reinares M, Daban C, Solé B, Rosa AR, Tabarés-Seisdedos R, Popovic D, Salamero M, Vieta E. Long-term outcome of cognitive impairment in bipolar disorder. *J Clin Psychiatry*. 2012 Jul;73(7):899-905.

Treuer T, Tohen M. Predicting the course and outcome of bipolar disorder: A review. *European Psychiatry*. 2010;25:328–333.

Ulloa RE, Birmaher B, Axelson D, Williamson DE, Brent, Ryan ND, Bridge J, Baugher M. Psychosis in a pediatric mood and anxiety disorders clinic: phenomenology and correlates. *J Am Acad Child Adolesc Psychiatry*. 2000 Mar;39(3):337-45.

Vallès V, Van Os J, Guillamat R, Gutiérrez B, Campillo M, Gento P, Fañanás L. Increased morbid risk for schizophrenia in families of in-patients with bipolar illness. *Schizophr Res.* 2000 Apr 7;42(2):83-90

Van Os, Takei N, Castle DJ, Wessely S, Der G, Murray RM. Premorbid aabnormalities in mania, schizomania, acute schizophrenia and cronic schizophrenia. *Soc Psychiatry Psychiatr Epidemiol* 1995; 30: 274-278.

Vega P, Barbeito S, de Azúa SR, Martínez-Cengotitabengoa M, González-Ortega I, Saenz M, González-Pinto A. Bipolar disorder differences between genders: special considerations for women. *Womens Health* (Lond Engl). 2011 Nov;7(6):663-74

Vega WA, Karno M, Alegria M, Alvidrez J, Bernal G, Escamilla M, Escobar J, Guarnaccia P, Jenkins J, Kopelowicz A, Lagomasino IT, Lewis-Fernandez R, Marin H, Lopez S, Loue S. Research issues for improving treatment of U.S. Hispanics with persistent mental disorders. *Psychiatr Serv*. 2007; 58:385–394.

Velakoulis D, Pantelis C, McGorry PD, Dudgeon P, Brewer W, Cook M, Desmond P, Bridle N, Tierney P, Murrie V, Singh B, Copolov D. Hippocampal volume in first-episode psychoses and chronic schizophrenia: a high-resolution magnetic resonance imaging study. *Arch Gen Psychiatry* 1999; 56:133-41.

Wald D, Lerner J: Lithium in the treatment of periodic catatonia: a case report. *Am J Psychiatry* 1978, 135:751–752.

Watsona DR, Andersonb J, Baic F et al. A voxel based morphometry study investigating brain structural changes in first episode psicosis. *Behavioural Brain Research* 227. 2012; 91–99.

Weiler MA, Fleisher MH, McArthur-Campbell D. Insight and symptom change in schizophrenia *Schizophr Res*. 2000 Sep 29; 45(1-2):29-36.

Winokur C, Clayton PJ, Reich T. *Manic depressive illness*. St Louis: CV Mosby, 1969

Winokur G, Coryell W, Keller M, Endicott J, Leon A. A family study of manic-depressive (bipolar I) disease. Is it a distinct illness separable from primary unipolar depression?. *Arch Gen Psychiatry*. 1995 May;52(5):367-73.

Winokur G, Black D, Nasrallah A. The schizoaffective continuum: non psychotic, mood- congruent and mood-incongruent. In: Marneros A, Tsuang MT (eds), *Schizoaffective and affective disorders: similarities and differences* (pp. 23 – 32). New York: Spring er Velag, 1990.

Winokur G, Scharfetter C, Agst J. A family study of psychotic symptomatology in schizophrenia, schizoaffective disorder, unipolar depression and bipolar disorder. *Eur Arch Psychiatr Neurol Sci*. 1985;234:295-298.

World Health Organization, 1993. The ICD-10 classification of mental and behavioural disorders, *Diagnostic Criteria for Research*. WHO, Geneva.

Yen CF, Chen CS, Ko CH et al. Changes in insight among patients with bipolar I disorder: a 2-year prospective study. *Bipolar Disord* 2007; 9: 238– 242.

Young LT, Bagby MR, Cooke RG, Parker JDA, Levitt AJ, Joffe RT. A comparison of Tridimensional Personality Questionnaire dimensions in bipolar patients and unipolar depression. *Psychiatry Research* 1995;58:139–143.

Young RC, Biggs JT, Siegler VE, et al.: A rating scale for mania: reliability, validity, and sensitivity. *Br J Psychiatry* 1978, 133:429–435.

Young RC, Schreiber MT, Nysewander RW. Psychotic mania. *Biol Psychiatry.* 1983 Oct;18(10):1167-73.

In: Affective Disorders
Editor: Linda D. Hambrick
ISBN: 978-1-62618-402-2

Chapter 2

THE RISK OF SUICIDAL BEHAVIORS IN AFFECTIVE DISORDERS

P. Mendez-Bustos[1], V. de Leon-Martinez[2] and J. Lopez-Castroman[2,3,*]

[1]Department of Psychology, Catholic University of Maule, Talca, Chile
[2]IIS-Fundación Jiménez Díaz, CIBERSAM, Madrid, Spain
[3]INSERM unit 1061, Montpellier, France

ABSTRACT

Affective disorders and suicidal behaviors are closely linked. They are among the most important public health problems in the western world. One million people may die every year as a consequence of self-inflicted harm. Moreover, it is estimated that 9 to 36 million people attempt suicide every year.

Within this population of suicide attempters, the prevalence of mental disorders is extremely high. The most frequent diagnosis among subjects who have completed suicide, according to psychological autopsies, is affective disorders. Specifically, bipolar disorder has been repeatedly reported as the mental disorder with the highest risk for completed suicide.

---

* Corresponding author: Jorge Lopez Castroman; Inserm U1061 – Hôpital La Colombière, Pavillon 42, 39 av. Charles Flauhault – B.P. 34493, 34093 Montpellier, Cedex 5, France. Tel: 33 (0) 499614560. E-mail: jorgecastroman@gmail.com.

In this chapter we will analyze the current epidemiological data concerning the relationship between affective disorders and the suicidal spectrum, including suicidal ideation, attempted suicide and completed suicide. We will also examine the association of affective disorders with specific subpopulations of suicide attempters, such as frequent attempters. In addition, we will analyze the influence of sociodemographic and economic variables on the development of these types of behaviors. Finally, we will introduce some of the available pharmacological treatment options and preventive strategies that have been applied to diminish the risk of suicidal behaviors among populations affected by affective disorders.

1. INTRODUCTION

Suicide remains a significant social and public health problem worldwide. It is estimated that nearly one million people die each year by suicide; one death every 40 seconds [1]. In Europe, suicide has become the leading cause of premature deaths especially in young adults [2, 3]. When comparing uncompleted suicide attempts and completed suicides, the statistics are even more alarming. It is estimated that attempted suicide can be up to 40 times more frequent than completed suicide [4]. According to Bertolote et al. [5] an estimated 9 to 36 million people attempt suicide each year. In addition, the individuals executing these types of behaviors are at a higher risk of repeating attempts and successfully completing suicide when compared to the general population [6-8]. Some authors have suggested that more than 2% of those who attempt suicide will die during the following year by their own hand and 7% within 10 years [9, 10].

On the other hand, mental disorders are a prevalent cause of burden at the population level. More than a third of the European population suffers from a mental disorder every year [11]. Most mental disorders increase suicide risk as reflected by their extremely high prevalence within the suicide attempter population [8]. Empirical evidence suggests that over 90% of suicide victims have one or more psychiatric disorders and contribute to 47-74% of the population at risk for suicide [12-14]. The association between psychiatric disorders and suicidal behaviors is particularly frequent in affective disorders. For example, affective disorders, especially major depressive disorder and bipolar disorder, are the most common psychiatric illnesses linked with suicide and are responsible for about 60% of all suicides [15-17].

Affective disorders are one of the most disabling and important contributors to the total burden of disease [18]. For instance, in the U.S. approximately 16% of adults will experience major depression in their lifetime [19]. The costs associated with affective disorders include direct medical costs due to hospitalization but also indirect costs due to absenteeism, loss of work productivity or suicidal behaviors. In 2010, the cost of affective disorders was estimated to be 113.4 billion euros in Europe [20]. In the U.S., the estimated cost for depression was calculated to be 83.1 billion dollars in 2000 [21] and the annual cost derived from bipolar I and bipolar II disorders was recently estimated at 151.0 billion dollars [22]. As for the cost of suicidal behavior, there are five hospitalizations and 22 visits to outpatient clinics for every suicide in the U.S. In addition, suicide is estimated to cost 1.8 billion each year due to lost productivity [23]. Suicidal behaviors convey large economic consequences for the mental health system [24]. Overall, suicide is responsible for 1.30% of the worldwide economic burden and 2% of the burden in Europe [25].

2. Suicidal Behavior and Affective Disorders

Affective disorders, substance misuse, anxiety disorders, personality disorders, and psychotic disorders have been considered risk factors for suicidal behavior [26]. Specifically, the results of some studies have demonstrated a greater lethality of suicidal behaviors in mood-disordered patients and elevated mortality rates from suicide [27, 28]. In the past decades authors have reported that 15% to 19% of the deaths in individuals diagnosed with a major affective disorder were due to suicide [29, 30]. A study using the U.S. National Comorbidity Survey Replication (NCS-R) found an odds ratio (OR) for a lifetime suicide attempts of over 5.0 among mood-disordered individuals [31]. Bipolar disorder was the pathology with the highest OR for suicide attempts (OR=6.7). The results of this survey also demonstrated that this psychiatric comorbidity was associated with an increased severity for consecutive attempts.

The risk of suicidal behaviors in affective disorders is mainly associated with major mood episodes, such as major depressive episodes or dysphoric mania, but rarely with euthymic or hyperthymic states [32].

In mood-disorder patients, self-harm behaviors and suicide attempts, are particularly associated with the risk of an eventual suicide [33, 34]. For instance, Tondo et al. [40] studied a sample of 2826 Italian (Sardinia) patients with major affective disorders and identified a suicide rate 8.2 times higher in these subjects than in the general population. The time sequence and development of suicidal behaviors, from suicidal ideation or suicidal behavior to completed suicide, is dependent on the type of disorder. Researchers suggest that, unlike personality disorders and psychotic disorders, depressive disorders accelerate this sequence [35, 36]. Interestingly, while depression seems to increase the desire for death, impulsiveness and poor behavioral control associated with bipolar disorder may particularly increase the probability of suicidal acts [31]. Furthermore, over 15% of the patients hospitalized for this type of pathology eventually commit suicide [37].

It should be noted as well that mood disorders significantly reduce the quality of life [38]. Two-thirds of individuals with depression report greater daily life impairments when compared to individuals suffering from chronic physical conditions [39].

2.1. Major Depressive Disorder (MDD)

Depression affects about one in five individuals during their lifetime, and is the fourth leading cause of disease burden in the world. It accounts for 4.5% of the worldwide total disease burden [41, 42]. The lifetime prevalence estimated for MDD is 16.2% with a higher cumulative prevalence in the age range between 18-59 years old. Sociodemographic factors such as unemployment, disability, low income, being previously married, or living in or near poverty are associated with a depressed mood [19]. Moreover, depression has been considered the leading cause of disability in the world due to its chronic and recurrent course. It is associated with physical impairment, severe impact on social skills, and unnatural deaths [43]. It accounts for 10.7% of the total years lived with disability [44].

Depression is also one of the most important risk factors for suicide attempts [45]. The mortality risk for suicide is markedly higher among depressed individuals than in the general population; over 50% of all people who die by suicide meet criteria for a depressive disorder [1, 12, 43]. A pioneer study that followed patients with MDD for 30 to 40 years found that 10.6% of patients had eventually committed suicide [46]. Other authors have reported suicide rates that vary between 2.7% and 20% in depressed samples [30, 47, 48].

Regarding psychiatric comorbidity, the analysis of the NCS-R demonstrated that 72.1% of the individuals who had experienced MDD in their lifetime met the criteria for at least one other mental disorder [19]. This frequent comorbidity increases the risk of suicidal behavior. For instance, severe depression can increase the risk of suicide in patients with anxiety disorder [49]. In addition, patients with a major depressive episode and cyclothymic personality are more likely to have suicidal ideation and attempts during their lifetime [50, 51]. Nevertheless, depression and alcohol abuse disorders are the most important risk factors for suicide in Europe and North America [1, 52].

Clinical and psychosocial risk factors such as history of previous suicide attempts, high levels of hopelessness, guilt, impulsivity, chronic physical illness, childhood history of physical or sexual abuse and low self-esteem increase the likelihood of suicide in patients with a major depressive episode [33, 34, 53]. This list of factors shows an interrelationship between social, psychological and biological factors that agrees with the postulates of the Stress-Diathesis model. According to this model, stressful events frequently trigger suicidal crises, but individuals with a specific vulnerability may be more prone to suicidal behaviors when facing major difficulties [54]. Therefore, some of the major facilitating factors for suicide may be part of a long-lasting diathesis (vulnerability).

Early recognition and adequate treatment of depression is essential to for the prevention of suicidal behaviors [55, 56]. The Perfect Depression Care program of the Behavioral Health Services (BHS) has demonstrated that improving diagnosis and treatment MDD through the optimization of a healthcare system can significantly reduce rates of suicide and suicide attempts [57].

2.2. Bipolar Disorder (BD)

BD is a common and severe illness associated with a high risk of suicide [58, 59]. In a study on the bipolar spectrum performed in the U.S. population, the lifetime prevalence estimated was 1.0% for BD type I (manic and depression episodes), 1.1% for BD type II (hypomanic and depression episodes) and 4.4% for any BD. In a later study which involved 11 countries of American, European and Asian continents, the lifetime prevalence rates were 0.6% for BD type I disorder, 0.4% for BD type II disorder, and 2.4% if all bipolar spectrum disorders were considered [60, 61].

The most serious consequences of BD are suicidal attempts, which occur in nearly 55% of bipolar patients. BD shows the highest OR for a lifetime history of suicidal acts and the highest lethality compared with any other psychiatric disorder [40, 62]. Approximately 10% to 18% of patients with BD die by suicide [8, 27, 63]. Suicidal behavior frequently occurs early in the course of the illness and may be more common in BD type II than in BD type I [64]. Other studies have also found that BD type II has the highest suicide risk of all subtypes of major mood disorders [65, 66]. Moreover, the severity of suicidal behavior seems to increase monotonically from subthreshold BD to other BD types [61]. As with MDD patients, psychiatric comorbidity increases the risk of attempting and completing suicide in bipolar patients [67].

In the fields of clinical practice and prevention, it is often underlined that BD represents a devastating risk factor for both suicide attempts and completed suicide [68]. Empirical evidence has demonstrated that suicidal behavior is much more lethal in bipolar disorder than in the general population [69, 70]. One suicide is committed for every 30 attempts in the general population of the U.S. while this rate increases to one suicide for every 2-3 attempts among BD patients [70]. Early studies already showed that the suicide rates in bipolar patients were 24 to 30-fold higher than in the general population [29, 71]. Currently, other authors have confirmed these findings. Patients with bipolar and unipolar disorders have an increased risk for suicide (HR=3.5 men y HR=2.5 women). Estimates indicate a 20-fold higher risk of suicide in BD patients than in the general population [72, 73]. According to studies published between 1945 and 2001, the global suicide rate among BD individuals per year is significantly higher (0.395%) than the international base rate in the general population (0.0143%) [59]. Suicidal behaviors, including attempts and completed suicide, also seem to be more prevalent in BD subjects than among MDD subjects in out-patients care [40].

Other aspects to consider are the influences of different mood episodes on the suicidal risk of BD patients. A suicide autopsy study conducted by Isometsa et al. [17] on a group of 31 bipolar patients found that 79% of the suicides occurred during a depressive phase and 11% during a mixed episode. In another study, researchers found that 54.5% of patients had committed suicide during a mixed episode in contrast to only 2% during a pure manic episode [74].

Other authors have found that bipolar patients have a higher likelihood of suicidal behavior during pure or mixed depressive episodes [75, 76]. A depressive episode is usually the final mood episode prior to suicide in a majority of bipolar individuals. In general, the latest research indicates that during severe, pure or mixed depressive episodes between 78-89% of bipolar patients develop suicidal behavior [32, 77, 78].

Dunner and Fieve [79] defined "rapid cycling" as the presence of four or more manic or depressive episodes per year in bipolar patients. Between 13% and 56% of patients diagnosed with BD are rapid cyclers [80, 81], and they have been associated with a depressive onset of the BD. But most importantly, rapid cyclers also have an increased risk of attempting suicide [82], as well as making more frequent and more lethal suicide attempts than non-rapid cycling bipolar patients [67, 83].

Comorbidity is extremely frequent among bipolar patients. Some studies found that 65-71% of bipolar patients presented at least one comorbid psychiatric disorder, 42% two or more, and 24% three or more [69, 88]. High rates of Axis I and Axis II comorbidity in bipolar patients have been known to increase the risk of suicide [85].

Bipolar patients with comorbid psychiatric and personality disorders report previous suicide attempts more often [89-91]. This finding may be related to the different psychological characteristics of bipolar patients with and without comorbid disorders. Comorbid patients report higher scores in hopelessness, impulsivity or aggression, and lower scores in self-esteem or problem-solving skills [92].

Overall, researchers agree that the presence of multiple disorders or psychiatric comorbidity greatly increases the risk of suicide [90, 91, 93, 94]. In addition, bipolar patients with early onset of bipolar illness, prior history of suicide attempts, family history of suicide and suicide attempts, hopelessness, prior psychiatric hospitalizations, early sexual abuse, Cluster B personality disorder, increased number of prior psychiatric hospitalizations, alcohol abuse and other psychiatric comorbidity have an increased risk of suicide attempts and completed suicide [8, 84-87].

Several studies have noted that early recognition of bipolar disorder improves prognosis. This is particularly important due to the impact of the illness on daily life functioning and the benefits of early treatment. Early recognition reduces suicide risk and the detrimental effects of unsuitable treatments [84].

Suicide, substance abuse, and iatrogenic complications are among some of the clinical consequences of undiagnosed BD. Moreover, patients suffer a remarkable diminution in their quality of life, important socio-economic costs and may have a higher risk of suicide than patients with any other psychiatric or medical illness [95, 96].

3. Suicidal Behavior: A Multifactorial Analysis

Suicide is a complex multidimensional behavior that is influenced by psychological, biological, economic and socio-demographic factors [25, 31]. The lifetime prevalence of suicide ideation varies between 2.1% and 14.1%, while the lifetime prevalence of suicide plans varies between 1.4% and 9.8%. In addition, annual suicide rates in WHO countries vary between 0.4 and 20.3 per 100 000 [97].

The most commonly observed associations between suicide and sociodemographic variables are: a) male gender, as suicide risk is 3 to 4 times higher in men than in women [98, 99]; b) single, separated or widowed marital status; c) ages between 20 and 40 years old; and d) unemployment. The influence and impact of these factors vary depending upon the life stage of the subject [98, 100, 101].

In recent years there has been a marked increase in the incidence of suicide, specifically in ages 15-44 years old [102-104]. Suicide is the third leading cause of death in the world for this age range and the second for the 15-19 age group [105]. Countries like China, Japan and Mexico have seen significant increases. For instance, suicides have increased 275% in Mexico in the last 30 years [102, 106, 107]. Researchers estimate that 25% of the individuals who attempt suicide will attempt again within 10 years and 10% will die as a direct result of suicide [108]. Furthermore, by the year 2020 it is estimated that 1.53 million people will die from suicide and there will be 10-30 times more suicide attempts. On average a suicide will be completed every 20 seconds with a suicide attempt occurring every 1-2 seconds [109].

3.1. Socioeconomic Influences

Both the characteristics and the environment of an individual have been recognized as joint influences in regards to suicidal behavior. Durkheim [110] suggested that suicidal acts are a reflection of the characteristics of social changes and the society in which they occur. Thus, this type of behavior is more common in areas with increased social fragmentation, socioeconomic deprivation and devaluation of human capital. Factors such as unemployment, reduced income, divorce, birth rate, and membership in a particular social group have been associated with suicide [111, 112]. Moreover, there is a greater risk of suicidal behavior when people loose and/or are detached from their social support groups [99, 113].

Globalization and recent underlying economic changes have influenced the psychological and social dimensions of society. Stiglitz [114] proposed that the purpose of economic activity is to improve the welfare of the people. This improvement is reflected in indicators such as the Gross Domestic Product, the Consumer Price Index, the Human Development Index, unemployment rates and suicide rates, among others. Thus it stands to reason that higher prevalence and incidence of suicidal behavior have been identified in periods of economic crisis [115, 116]. Various authors have presented evidence of a procyclical relationship between a country's economy and suicide mortality [117, 118]. However, contrasting opinions identify a relationship between suicide and economic crises as countercyclical, increasing during recessions [103, 119].

The economic downturn that currently affects many countries in the world has become a source of psychological distress [98, 106, 120]. For instance, the prevalence of MDD in Greece rose from 3.3 in 2008 to 8.2 in 2011. Tthe recent increase in Greek and Italian suicide rates may reflect the negative impact of financial crises on mental health [121, 122]. In a context of economic crisis there is a deterioration of working conditions, increased workload, reduced income, and rising unemployment. These factors are directly correlated with the demand for attention in mental health facilities, the admission rates at psychiatric units and the number of psychiatric diagnoses given [123, 124]. From a clinical standpoint, some authors have found an association between job loss and mental health indicators such as greater psychological distress; depressive, anxious and psychosomatics symptoms [125, 126]; more frequent major depression episodes [127]; alcohol misuse [128, 129); and suicidal behaviors [126, 130]. In conclusion, there exists some consensus among researchers about the consequences generated by an economic crisis, especially with regards to its negative effect on mental health [126]. The augmented risk of presenting an affective disorder in times of crisis supports the need to strengthen healthcare spending on primary care and suicide prevention programs.

3.2. Suicide Reattempters (SR)

Individuals who have attempted suicide are at an increased risk for recurrent suicidal behavior [131-133] and are more likely to complete suicide [134, 135]. Each time an individual attempts suicide, the risk for a reattempt increases by 32% [136]. Actually, 20% to 70% of the individuals who kill themselves may have attempted suicide previously [137]; therefore, suicide reattempts are fairly common.

Ruengorn et al. [133] and Spirito et al. [138] found that 40% of suicide attempters made a new attempt 30-90 days after leaving hospitalized care. Over 1-2 years the repetition rate decreases to 14-25% of the population [139-141]. Follow-up studies ranging from 4-10 years showed that rates of repeated suicide attempts occur at even higher rates: 20-55% [142-144]. As is evident, repetition rates can vary greatly depending on the population of attempters that is being analyzed and period of follow-up. However, since suicide attempts are considered to be the strongest single predictor of subsequent completed suicide, it is vital to accurately identify the factors that can predict the recurrence of these attempts and to distinguish repeaters from non-repeaters [145].

3.2.1. Clinical and Psychological Variables

In regards to major clinical variables associated with reattempters, these individuals are more likely to present a family history of psychiatric problems, as well as affective disorders such as MDD, dysthymia, depressive mood, BD, and other psychiatric diagnoses [135, 140, 146]. Other factors associated with the repetition of suicide attempts include prior attempts, high suicidal ideation and lethality, family history of suicidal behavior, history of psychiatric treatment and high levels of impulsivity [139, 147-149]. In addition, repeated suicide attempts have been linked with a history of emotional, physical and sexual abuse [148, 150, 151]. Psychological factors related to the repetition of suicidal behavior include low values on active handling and comforting cognitions, high scores in passive reactions, emotional dysregulation, greater exposure to stressful life events, poor coping conflict strategies, interpersonal dependency, low sense of self-efficiency, poor family relations and low global functioning [147, 152, 153].

3.3. Gender and Age Aspects of Suicidal Behavior

3.3.1. The Gender Paradox

Epidemiological studies performed in diverse cultures and countries show gender differences in suicidal behavior. Women make more suicide attempts [154]; however, men commit suicide at a higher rate [9]. In developed countries, completed suicides are 2 to 4-fold more frequent among men [99, 155] while suicide attempts are 2 to 3-fold more frequent among women [94,

156]. In fact, the suicide rates increase with age in both genders while at the same time the attempted/completed suicide ratio decreases [157, 158]. However, the differential distribution of suicidal behavior by gender, known as the gender paradox, is not found in all countries. In rural China, women commit suicide at an equal or greater rate than men [159-161]. In India and Kuwait, suicide rates are also similar between men and women [154]. Variations of the gender paradox in non-western countries, such as those mentioned, could be due to the greater lethality of the methods used by these women in these parts of the world; for instance, self-burning practices in India and the use of pesticides in China. These cultural differences may account for a greater rate of completed suicides in these populations [162, 163].

Proposed explanations for the gender paradox are based on the use of different suicidal methods which influence lethality and cultural characteristics of suicide attempts [155, 164]. Firstly, males have greater levels of aggression, more substance use disorders, and apply violent suicide methods more frequently, such as shooting by firearm, hanging or suffocation. In contrast, females generally attempt poisoning, wrist cutting or falling from heights [92, 165]. Furtermore, males seek social support and specific help for their problems less often [166] and appear to be more affected by external factors and social demands than females [101, 104]. The differences in the prevalence of affective disorders, BD being more frequent among men and MDD more frequent among women, support the existence of gender differences in suicidal behavior [167]. In fact, bipolar males are at greater risk for completing suicide but attempt suicide less often than females [70].

It is worthy to note that although the gender paradox clearly exists in most countries, over time changes in the frequency of suicide rates could alter this perception. For instance, Gunnel et al. (2003) showed that although the suicide rate in England and Wales is still higher in men than in women, the gender gap has decreased in recent years (1950-1998). In addition, female suicide rates in some developed countries have augmented over time [98]. For example, female suicide rates in South Korea have increased from 1.1 (1986) to 4.2 (2005) per 100.000 [168]. The gender rate of completed suicide in the U.S. has remained stable around 2.5:1 (completed suicide is 2.5 fold more frequent in men than women) from 1930 to 1971, but has increased ever since reaching a proportion of 4.4:1 in the last years of the nineties [169].

3.3.2. Suicide Along the Life Cycle

Infantile suicide is an unusual occurrence; however, the number of suicides among children and adolescents till the age of 14 appears to be increasing in several countries. Rates vary from 0 to 3.1 per 100000 with an estimated 0.6 per 100000 global rate and a 2:1 male/female coefficient [170]. These rates increase later on in adolescence due to greater planning and more lethal suicide attempts together with a higher prevalence of mental disorders and substance abuse [165, 171].

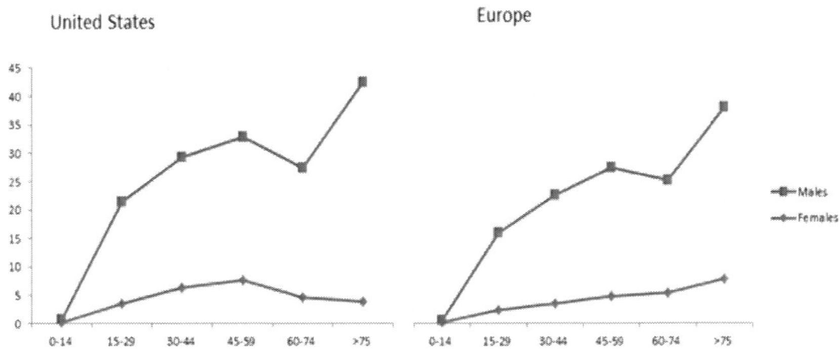

Source: http://data.euro.who.int/hfamdb, http://webappa.cdc.gov/sasweb/ncipc/mortrate10_us.html.

Figure 1. Evolution of suicide rates by gender and age groups in the general population of the United States and Europe 1999-2010.

Suicide is the third leading cause of death for the age groups of 10-14 years old and 15-24 years old, as well as the second leading cause for persons 25-34 years olds in the U.S. [172]. In Europe, it is the second leading cause of mortality after accidental deaths (173). Bridge et al. (2006) confirmed affective disorders as a major risk factor for adolescents in both genders. While no significant different in the prevalence of MDD was found in the 8-13 age group between males and females [174], female suicide risk increases around puberty and is associated with the more frequent onset of depressive episodes [175, 176]. Young women may be particularly exposed to suicidal risk [94, 177]. An abrupt increase in the risk of suicidal ideation, plans and attempts is seen in adolescent women from the age of 13 [178].

The rates of suicidal ideation and attempts consistently increase after puberty in females when compared to male adolescents [179, 180]. Saunders and Hawton [181] suggested that the initiation of menstruation is the moment when gender differences in the ratios of affective disorders and suicidal behavior move apart. The highest rates of suicide attempts appear earlier in adolescent women when compared to men by a time gap of about 3 years [182]. In addition, adolescent females who committed suicide had more previous attempts and more frequent conflicts with their parents than their male counterpart [171, 183]. Adolescent women, who commit suicide, may use increasingly violent methods, such as shooting by firearms or hanging [171]. This increase in lethality could signify a reduction in the gender difference of suicide rates [9] although by the age of 19 the risk for men and women is similar [184]. A study of 10-24 years old subjects found that 81% of suicide victims were males and 19% were females [172].

Suicide is the second leading cause of deaths in 25-34 years olds after accidental deaths in the U. S. and Europe [172, 185]. The suicide rate was 2.4 times higher among young adults when compared with adolescents in a study on several western countries [186]. Suicide rates increase continuously from adolescence until peaking around 45-59 years (Figure 1). This population, representing the economically active population, is particularly exposed to work pressure and environmental demands. According to the stress-diathesis model, the incorporation of women to the labor market may have led this group to greater suicide risk [54, 187, 188]. In addition, the influence of marital status should be considered for this age group, as being married is a protective factor. However, those who are single, divorced or widowed have an increased risk of suicidal behavior independently of gender [189, 190]. Divorced women present lower suicide rates after divorce than men, but the gender protection seems to decrease with advancing age [191].

Both in the U.S. and Europe, the highest suicide rates were observed in the 45-59 years group and among the elderly (older than 75 years) in 2010 (Figure 1). However, within the U.S. the age of the peak of incidence in the 45-59 years group increased while the age of the second peak among the elderly decreased between 1999 and 2010. In Europe the age of both peaks of incidence decreased during the same period [192, 193].

Advancing age seems to increase the divergence between sexes when considering the rates of completed suicide in the elderly population [156]. Whereas suicide attempt rates diminish with age independently of gender [194], the rates of completed suicide augment with age. This increase is particularly prominent among men [195] reaching rates 6-12 times higher than women in western countries [196]. This important difference has been attributed to better planning, fewer warnings of suicidal intent and the use of more lethal methods in men, such as, the use of firearms and hanging/suffocation [197, 198].

In Eastern Europe and South America, on the other hand, the male to female suicide ratio has not changed in individuals over the age of 65 [199] and it has even decreased in the U.S. [94]. Suicide statistics in the U.S.

indicate that the highest male suicide risk appears in individuals 85 years old or older, while the highest female suicide risk appears in the 60-64 age group. It appears while male suicide rate increases with age, female suicide risk appears to be more stable.

Most suicide victims 60 years or older were followed in mental health settings and diagnosed with either Depression/Dysthymia (males=80.8% and females=79.1%) or BD (males=6.2% and females=11.1%) in the U.S. [196].

3.3.3. Postpartum, Maternity and Menopause

Different authors support the idea that the birth of a child is a protective factor against fatal and non-fatal self-harm especially in the first year after delivery [200]. Regardless, suicide is the fourth leading cause of maternal deaths in the world [201] and the leading cause of death in first-year postpartum women in the United Kingdom [202]. Gissler et al. [203] found that suicide rates associated with childbirth were close to half of those among non-pregnant women aged 15-49 years, but that adolescent mothers were three times more likely to commit suicide than other females in their age group.

This protective factor differs in pregnant women with psychiatric disorders. Between 10-25% of pregnant and postpartum women experience depressive disorders [204, 205] or anxiety disorders [206, 207]. These women are more likely to complete suicide, especially during the first months after childbirth [203, 208]. The risk of suicide was calculated to be 70 times higher in women with psychiatric disorders during the first year after childbirth when compared to the general female population [200]. Moreover, pregnant teens represent a high-risk group, with an estimated 16-44% prevalence rate of depression [209, 210].

In the US, female suicide is concentrated in women 35-64 years old (64.8%) with rates peaking at 9.1/100000 in women 45-54 years old; the age range typically associated with menopause [172].

Similar results have been reported in England and Wales [104]. Social changes have resulted in many women in this age group becoming economically active, and thus maybe increasing the risk of suicide and mental health problems [211, 212].

Additionally, depression and suicidal ideation have been associated with the perimenopause phase in women when compared to premenopausal and postmenopausal [213]. From the age of 50, suicide rates among women tend to diminish progressively till old age [156].

4. Preventive Aspects

Considering the complex etiology of suicide, the identification of the specific factors associated with suicidal behavior is essential for its prevention [214]. There are over 450 million people diagnosed with mental disorders in the world [215] and, as previously discussed, suicidal risk increases in individuals with psychiatric disorders [216]. Up to 83% of suicides may be seen by a primary care physician a year before the patient's death and 66% the month before [217, 218]. However, only a third of mood-disorder individuals may use formal health services in the previous year of the onset of suicidal behavior and only half of those may receive adequate treatment [38].

In the same line, Gonda et al. [166] found that DSM-IV axis I mental illnesses are in general underdiagnosed, undertreated or inadequately treated. Likewise, over half of the bipolar patients that completed suicide were untreated at the time of their death [59, 219]. Preventive efforts should therefore be used to improve the quality of care, the screening for depressed patients in primary care settings and the education of health professionals on the treatment of mood disorders.

Suicide prevention involves a multidimensional approach that should incorporate not only the individual at risk, but also the family, relevant others, and the community in the prevention efforts.

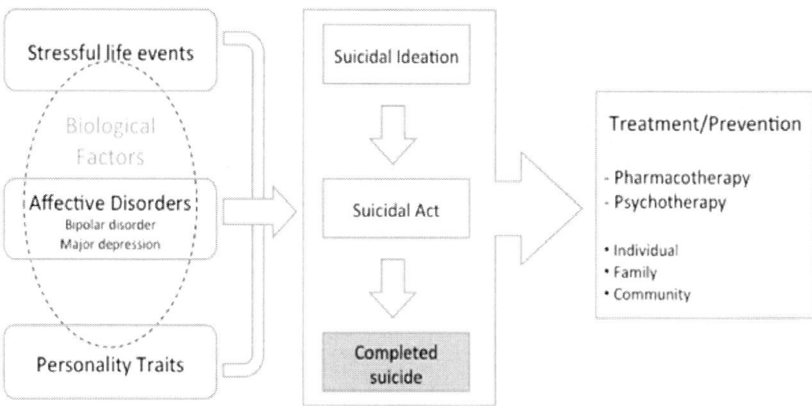

Figure 2. A model summarizing the relationship between suicidal behavior and affective disorders.

Five areas of suicide prevention have been highlighted as key to reducing risk and harm [220]: 1) Education and awareness programs for the general public and professionals (public education campaigns, training of primary care physicians, training of educators); 2) Screening methods for high-risk persons; 3) Treatment of psychiatric disorders (pharmacotherapy, psychotherapy); 4) Restricting access to lethal means (firearm, pesticides, etc.); and 5) Media reporting of suicide (internet, print and broadcast media).

Intervention programs are characterized by different theoretical orientations and design. Some of them are:

a) Cognitive Behavioral Programs and Models:
   - Dialectic Behavioral Therapy that includes three structured individual sessions and one group therapy per week during one year [221].
   - Brief therapy based on the Manual-assisted cognitive-behavior therapy (MACT) that includes 2-6 individual sessions [222].
   - Brief cognitive therapy focused on problems for 5 sessions during 3 months after the attempt.

b) Psychodynamic approaches:
   - Individual therapy with one weekly session, group therapy three times a week, expressive therapy in a partial hospitalization setting, and weekly community meetings for 18 months [223].
   - Strategies for problem solving with weekly training sessions in interpersonal skills and conflict resolution for about 5 months [224].
   - Psychodynamic interpersonal therapy consisting of 4 sessions in the patient's home by a nurse therapist [225].

c) Family interventions consisting of five sessions focused on the family and home environment [226].

d) Strategies and Multimodal Interventions
   - Psychosocial and Psychoeducational for individuals with Recurrent Suicide Attempts (PISA) comprising of group therapy format organized into 5 modules (emotional education, problem solving, crisis management and interpersonal relationship skills) that consist of at least 20 sessions of approximately 90 minutes. An interprofessional approach is favored in this intervention [227, 228].

e) Minimal Intervention approaches (case management programs):
   - The "green card," a phone number card that allows easy 24 hours communication with health care professionals [229].

- Brief Intervention and Contact (BIC) for suicide attempters [230] that includes standard 1 hour sessions followed by a contact period after discharge for information regarding the conditions of social and psychological stress, protective factors and risk of suicidal behavior. Follow-up monitoring is done via telephone or home visits in weeks 1, 2, 4, 7 and 11, and months 4, 6, 12 and 18 after discharge.
- The Baerum Model (231) a rapid-response intervention that seeks to improve adherence to treatment through specialized health care and community interventions. This model includes home visits, telephone calls and text messages over a period of six months.
- Perfect Depression Care Program of the Behavioral Health Services [57] whose main objective is to improve the diagnosis and treatment of MDD. Patients are evaluated and their suicide risk is classified (high, moderate, low), they attend weekly group therapy and have the option of accessing specific information through the program's website.
- "Crisis Card" used for first-attempters and provides patients a “resource card” with which they can communicate with a psychiatrist 24 hours a day [232].
- ALGOS algorithm is used to create a crisis management plan for each patient that analyses adherence and treatment compliance after a suicide attempt and seeks to reduce the number of suicide reattempters. Several strategies are established to support the patient: systematic telephone contact, custom postal shipments and use of the "crisis card" [233].
- "Connectedness" sending personalized letters to maintain contact with patients at risk to demonstrate that there are people worried about them. These are sent monthly for 4 months, then every 2 months for 8 months and finally every 3 months for 4 years [234].
- A similar intervention based on the strategy "connectedness" proposes sending systematic individualized postcards for a year during a patient’s follow-up after a suicide attempt [235].

Generally the above-mentioned programs seek to intervene in high risk populations, increase the access to mental health services, improve diagnosis and treatment of depression, and develop strategies for mental health care and education. They are generally led by interdisciplinary teams of mental health professionals (psychiatrists, nurses, psychologists, social workers) and perform patient follow-ups ranging from 4-18 months. Some intervention groups have used control groups, randomized controlled trials and comparisons of traditional treatments to evaluate their effectiveness. In addition, some interventions incorporate family members and significant others, as well as training in interpersonal skills. Although there is no clear evidence regarding the efficiency and effectiveness of these programs, they seem to act as protective factors, contributing to reduce the number of suicide attempts. Some intervention programs report a 22-73% reduction of suicide rates [236, 237]. Thus, it is crucial to expand the coverage of prevention programs, especially those focused on mood disorders.

In addition to individual and group preventive therapies, several countries have recognized the importance of developing and implementing national suicide prevention strategies; for example, implementing actions focused on high-risk individuals and incorporating other key social units such as family and community. The Finnish National Suicide Program [238] sought to decentralize intervention to other social sectors, such as religious groups, the police and other local development projects. The program finished with successful results and achieved a reduction in the suicide rate from 30 per 100,000 to 18 per 100,000.

The National Suicide Prevention Strategy for England [239], a national multi-sector intervention, is focused on reducing suicide in high-risk groups, promoting mental wellbeing, and reducing access to lethal means of suicide. The program aimed to reduce suicide by 20% by 2010 and during its first three years had achieved a reduction of 7.4%. Similarly, the Flemish suicide prevention program [240] aimed to achieve a reduction of 8% in the suicide rate between the years 2000 and 2010.

While many intervention methods exist, our knowledge of the prevention of suicidal behavior is still insufficient. Cross-national studies are a priority as not all research findings and intervention programs are applicable to different social contexts. Further research is needed to meet the particularity and specificity of different target populations. Even though studies have attempted to determine more accurately the factors involved in suicide and their influences, researchers agree on the need for further studies incorporating biological, social, psychological and cultural factors that allow for a better understanding of this serious public health problem. There is clear evidence of the risk associated to suicidal patients with mood disorders and thus a great need to intervene to reduce risk and suicide mortality.

5. Pharmacological Treatment

Suicide has become a major public health problem in the world. 56-87% of suicide victims and reattempters have major affective disorders [87, 241]. This figure explains the important rise in the prescription of antidepressants over the last decades [242]. For example, Martín Arias et al. [243] identified a 7-fold increase in the prescription of antidepressants from 1992 to 2005 in Spain. Empirical evidence suggests that selective serotonin reuptake inhibitors (SSRIs) decrease the risk of suicidal behavior in depressed patients more quickly than others types of antidepressants [244, 245], but other types of antidepressants have been effective in the reduction of suicide risk as well. The risk of suicide is reduced about 60% in patients taking lithium for mood disorders or MDD [246, 247]. Angst et al. [53] compared the variation of suicide risk in untreated mood disorder patients with those treated with lithium, neuroleptics and antidepressants during a 44 year follow-up. They found that all three treatments decreased mortality and risk of suicide, and that combined treatments were more effective than mono-therapy.

Overall, lithium and SSRIs have been found to be effective in decreasing suicide risk in patients with mood disorders. The main effects seem to be associated with the decreased aggressiveness and impulsiveness, clinical factors associated with the risk of suicidal behavior [248]. In addition, antidepressant treatment appears to mainly reduce the risk of future suicidal behavior after a previous attempt [249, 250]. It is still unclear if other mood-stabilizers or antipsychotics may decrease the risk of suicide, with the exception of clozapine that shows a specific antisuicidal effect apparently through the reduction of affective symptoms [251].

Despite advances in research, the relationship between antidepressants and risk of suicidal behavior remains unclear and debatable [242, 252]. The beneficial effect of these medications has been questioned as the increase in prescribing and use may encourage the development of suicidal behavior [253].

Some authors bring attention to the fact that pharmacotherapy is a risk in and of itself as subjects frequently use pharmacotherapy as a method to attempt suicide [245]. In England 20% of suicide deaths are due to antidepressant overdose as tricycle antidepressants are more toxic than SSRIs [254]. A study on 1329 cases of elderly people found a temporal difference in suicide risk when comparing patients who had received SSRI antidepressants to those using other antidepressants. The risk of suicide was five times higher during the first month of treatment but during the second and subsequent months there was not differential risk [255].

Although the effectiveness of SSRIs and tricyclic antidepressants has been demonstrated in adults, their positive effect is less clear in children and adolescents [256]. Some authors associated the use of SSRIs with an increased risk of suicidal ideation or non-fatal suicide attempts mainly in children and adolescents [256, 257].

The application and effectiveness of certain types of pharmacotherapy can be dependent on the clinical findings. Patients with bipolar or unipolar disorder or with mixed states of depression may require antidepressant therapy, mood stabilizers and/or atypical antipsychotics. Lack of treatment may result in the destabilization of the mood disorder, worsening of the depression, treatment resistance and/or, in some cases, appearance of suicidal behavior [258, 259].

There is agreement that lithium monotherapy reduces the risk of suicidal behaviors in bipolar patients and is more effective for the prevention of suicides and suicide attempts than other mood stabilizers, antidepressants and antipsychotic monotherapy [28, 53, 260]. The effectiveness of lithium has also been demonstrated in comparison with carbamazepine in BD [261] and in recurrent MDD [262]. In conclusion, the frequent combinations of pharmacological therapies in clinical practice increase the possibilities of finding differential effects between treatments.

Although both pharmacotherapy and long-term psychotherapy have been shown to reduce the risk of suicide in mood-disorder patients, some researchers recommend the use of antidepressants combined with psychological therapy to facilitate the monitoring of symptoms and the effects of pharmacological treatment, especially at the start of treatment [263].

CONCLUSION

Both affective disorders and suicidal behavior are prevalent and convey a large burden on both the society and the individual. They are both directly related and have huge economic and social consequences. Individuals with affective disorders are at risk for attempting and completing suicide. It is therefore important to optimize the performance of mental health care services to detect and treat people at risk as early as possible. In other words, early identification of risk and protective factors in patients with affective disorders may allow for the identification of specific risk groups that could be treated accordingly. Understanding and identifying the complex interaction of suicide risk factors within major depression episodes and bipolar illness would be a crucial tool for prediction and prevention. Although some prevention strategies have proven to be effective, there is insufficient empirical support for the generalization of their use. A systematic assessment of the impact and effectiveness of suicide prevention strategies is key to planning and improving future interventions. Planning, development and implementation of mental health programs could integrate the different dimensions that influence the appearance of suicidal behavior including individual, family and community approaches.

Acknowledgments

Pablo Mendez Bustos received funding for predoctoral studies by Fundacion Carolina, Madrid, Spain. Jorge Lopez-Castroman was supported by a Fondamental Foundation Grant.

References

[1] World Health Organization, *Suicide prevention (SUPRE)* 2003 [cited 2012 August 15]. Available from: http://www.who.int/mental_health/prevention/suicide/ suicideprevent/en/.

[2] Johannessen HA, Dieserud G, De Leo D, Claussen B, Zahl PH. Chain of care for patients who have attempted suicide: A follow-up study from Baerum, Norway. *BMC public health*. 2011;11:81.

[3] World Health Organization. *The Global Burden of Disease 2004* Update 2004 [cited 2012 July 21]. Available from: http://www.who.int/healthinfo/globalburdendisease/2004reportupdate/en/index.html.

[4] Schmidtke A, Bille-Brahe U, Deleo D, Kerkhof A, Bjerke T, Crepef P, et al. Attempted suicide in Europe: Rates, trends and sociodemographic characteristics of suicide attempters during the period 1989-1992. Results of the WHO/EURO Multicentre Study on Parasuicide. *Acta Psychiatrica Scandinavica*. 1996;93(5):327-38.

[5] Bertolote JM, Fleischmann A, Butchart A, Besbelli N. Suicide, suicide attempts and pesticides: A major hidden public health problem. *Bulletin of the World Health Organization*. 2006;84(4):260.

[6] Brådvik L, Berglund M. Aspects of the Suicidal Career in Severe Depression: A Comparison Between Attempts in Suicides and Controls. *Archives of Suicide Research.* 2002;6(4):339-49.

[7] Forman EM, Berk MS, Henriques GR, Brown GK, Beck AT. History of multiple suicide attempts as a behavioral marker of severe psychopathology. *The American Journal of Psychiatry.* 2004; 161(3): 437-43.

[8] Harris EC, Barraclough B. Suicide as an outcome for mental disorders. A meta-analysis. *The British Journal of Psychiatry.* 1997;170(3):205-28.

[9] Beautrais AL. Suicide and serious suicide attempts in youth: A multiple-group comparison study. *The American Journal of Psychiatry.* 2003; 160(6): 1093-9.

[10] Owens D, Horrocks J, House A. Fatal and non-fatal repetition of self-harm. Systematic review. *The British journal of psychiatry: The journal of mental science.* 2002; 181: 193-9.

[11] Andlin-Sobocki P, Jönsson B, Wittchen H-U, Olesen J. Cost of disorders of the brain in Europe. *European Journal of Neurology.* 2005;12:1-27.

[12] Cavanagh J, Carson, AJ., Sharpe,M., Lawrie, SM. Psychological autopsy studies of suicide: A systematic review. *Psychological Medicine.* 2003; 33(3):395-405.

[13] Hawton K, Hall S, Simkin S, Bale L, Bond A, Codd S, et al. Deliberate self-harm in adolescents: A study of characteristics and trends in Oxford, 1990-2000. *Journal of Child Psychology and Psychiatry.* 2003; 44(8): 1191-8.

[14] Mościcki EK. Identification of suicide risk factors using epidemiologic studies. *Psychiatric Clinics of North America.* 1997;20(3):499-517.

[15] Beautrais AL, Joyce PR, Mulder RT, Fergusson DM, et al. Prevalence and comorbidity of mental disorders in persons making serious suicide attempts: A case-control study. *The American Journal of Psychiatry.* 1996; 153(8):1009-14.

[16] Bertolote JM, Fleischmann A, De Leo D, Wasserman D. Suicide and mental disorders: Do we know enough? *The British Journal of Psychiatry.* 2003;183(5):382-3.

[17] Isometsa E, Henriksson MM, Aro HM, Lonnqvist JK Suicide in bipolar disorder in Finland. *The American Journal of Psychiatry.* 1994; 151(7): 1020.

[18] Wittchen HU, Holsboer F, Jacobi F. Met and unmet needs in the management of depressive disorder in the community and primary care:

The size and breadth of the problem. *The Journal of clinical psychiatry*. 2001;62 Suppl 26:23-8.

[19] Kessler RC; Berglund PD, O; Jin R, Koretz D, Merikangas KR, Rush AJ, Walters EE, Wang PS., The epidemiology of major depressive disorder: Results from the national comorbidity survey replication (ncs-r). *JAMA*. 2003;289(23):3095-105.

[20] Gustavsson A, Svensson M, Jacobi F, Allgulander C, Alonso J, Beghi E, et al. Cost of disorders of the brain in Europe 2010. *European Neuropsychopharmacology*. 2011;21(10):718-79.

[21] Greenberg P, Kessler, RC., Birnbaum, HG., Leong, SA., Lowe, SW., Berglund, PA. and Corey-Lisle, PK. The Economic Burden of Depression in the United States: How Did It Change Between 1990 and 2000? *J. Clin. Psychiatry* 2003;64:1465-75.

[22] Dilsaver SC. An estimate of the minimum economic burden of bipolar I and II disorders in the United States: 2009. *Journal of Affective Disorders*. 2011;129(1–3):79-83.

[23] Goldsmith SK PT, Kleinman AM, et al. eds,. *Reducing suicide: A national imperative* 2002.

[24] National Mental Health Information Center. Substance Abuse and Mental Health Services Administration. National Mental Health Information Center. *National Strategy for Suicide Prevention: Goals and objectives for action*. 2001 [cited 2012 March 19]. Available from: http://mentalhealth.samhsa.gov/publications/allpubs/SMA01-3517/ch7.asp.

[25] Andrés AR, Halicioglu F. Determinants of suicides in Denmark: Evidence from time series data. *Health Policy*. 2010;98(2-3):263-9.

[26] Bolton JM, Cox BJ, Afifi TO, Enns MW, Bienvenu OJ, Sareen J. Anxiety disorders and risk for suicide attempts: Findings from the Baltimore Epidemiologic Catchment Area follow-up study. *Depression and anxiety*. 2008;25(6):477-81.

[27] Angst F, Stassen HH, Clayton PJ, Angst J. Mortality of patients with mood disorders: Follow-up over 34–38 years. *Journal of Affective Disorders*. 2002;68(2–3):167-81.

[28] Baldessarini RJ, Tondo L, Davis P, Pompili M, Goodwin FK, Hennen J. Decreased risk of suicides and attempts during long-term lithium treatment: A meta-analytic review. *Bipolar Disorders*. 2006;8(5p2):625-39.

[29] Guze SB, Robins E. Suicide and Primary Affective Disorders. *The British Journal of Psychiatry*. 1970 October 1, 1970;117(539):437-8.

[30] Goodwin FKaJ, K.R. *Suicide in manic-depressive illness* Oxford University Press. New York1999.

[31] Nock MK, Hwang I, Sampson NA, Kessler RC. Mental disorders, comorbidity and suicidal behavior: Results from the National Comorbidity Survey Replication. *Mol. Psychiatry*. 2010;15(8):868-76.

[32] Rihmer Z. Suicide risk in mood disorders. *Current Opinion in Psychiatry*. 2007; 20(1): 17-22.

[33] Coryell WaY, EA. Clinical Predictors of Suicide in Primary Major Depressive Disorder. *The Journal of Clinical Psychiatry*. 2005;66:412-7.

[34] Oquendo M, Galfalvy, H., Russo, S., Ellis, SP., Grunebaum, MF., Burke, A. and Mann, JJ. Prospective Study of Clinical Predictors of Suicidal Acts After a Major Depressive Episode in Patients With Major Depressive Disorder or Bipolar Disorder. *The American Journal of Psychiatry*. 2004;161(8):1433-41.

[35] Angst J, Gamma A, Endrass J, Hantouche E, Goodwin R, Ajdacic V, et al. Obsessive-compulsive syndromes and disorders: Significance of comorbidity with bipolar and anxiety syndromes. *European archives of psychiatry and clinical neuroscience*. 2005; 255(1): 65-71.

[36] Runeson BS, Beskow J, Waern M. The suicidal process in suicides among young people. *Acta Psychiatrica Scandinavica*. 1996;93(1):35-42.

[37] Maris R. Suicide. *Lancet*. 2002;360:319–26.

[38] Alonso J, Angermeyer MC, Lépine JP. The European Study of the Epidemiology of Mental Disorders (ESEMeD) project: An epidemiological basis for informing mental health policies in Europe. *Acta Psychiatrica Scandinavica*. 2004; 109:5-7.

[39] Ormel J, Petukhova, M., Chaterji, S., Aguilar-Gaxiola, S., Alonso, J. et al. Disabilityand treatment of specific mental and physical disorders across the world: Result from the WHO World Mental Health Surveys. *The British Journal of Psychiatry*. 2008;192(5):368-75.

[40] Tondo L, Lepri B, Baldessarini RJ. Suicidal risks among 2826 Sardinian major affective disorder patients. *Acta Psychiatrica Scandinavica*. 2007; 116(6):419-28.

[41] Sullivan PF KR, Kendler KS. Latent class analysis of life-time depressive symptoms in the National Comorbidity Survey. *The American Journal of Psychiatry*. 1998; 155: 1398–406.

[42] World Health Organization. *WHO statistics part one: Ten statistical highlights in global public health* 2007 [cited 2012 March 19]. Available from: http://www.who.int/whosis/whostat200710highlights.

[43] Harris EC, Barraclough B. Excess mortality of mental disorder. *The British Journal of Psychiatry*. 1998;173(1):11-53.

[44] Üstün TB, Ayuso-Mateos JL, Chatterji S, Mathers C, Murray CJL. Global burden of depressive disorders in the year 2000. *The British Journal of Psychiatry*. 2004; 184(5): 386-92.

[45] Bernal M, Haro JM, Bernert S, Brugha T, de Graaf R, Bruffaerts R, et al. Risk factors for suicidality in Europe: Results from the ESEMED study. *Journal of Affective Disorders*. 2007;101(1–3):27-34.

[46] Winokur G T, M. T*he Iowa 500: Suicide in mania, depression, and schizophrenia*. 1975; 132(6):650-1.

[47] Fredman L SV, Kaplan BH et al. The association between depressive symptoms and mortality among older participants in the Epidemiologic Catchment Area-Piedmont Health Survey. *The Journals of Gerontology*. 1989; 44(4): S149-S56.

[48] Zheng D MC, Croft JB, Giles WH, Davis D, Scott WK. Major depression and all-cause mortality among white adults in the United States. *Annals of Epidemiology*. 1997; 7(3): 213-8.

[49] Hawgood J, De Leo D. Anxiety disorders and suicidal behaviour: An update. *Current Opinion in Psychiatry*. 2008;21(1):51-64.

[50] Akiskal HS, Benazzi F. Psychopathologic correlates of suicidal ideation in major depressive outpatients: Is it all due to unrecognized (bipolar) depressive mixed states? *Psychopathology*. 2005; 38(5):273-80.

[51] Kochman FJ, Hantouche EG, Ferrari P, Lancrenon S, Bayart D, Akiskal HS. Cyclothymic temperament as a prospective predictor of bipolarity and suicidality in children and adolescents with major depressive disorder. *Journal of Affective Disorders*. 2005;85(1–2):181-9.

[52] Oquendo M, Chaudhury, S. and Mann, J. Pharmacotherapy of Suicidal Behavior in Bipolar Disorder. *Archives of Suicide Research*. 2005; 9(3): 237-50.

[53] Angst J, Angst F, Gerber-Werder R, Gamma A. Suicide in 406 Mood-Disorder Patients With and Without Long-Term Medication: A 40 to 44 Years' Follow-Up. *Archives of Suicide Research*. 2005;9(3):279-300.

[54] Mann JJ. Neurobiology of suicidal behaviour. *Nature Reviews Neuroscience*. 2003; 4(10): 819-28.

[55] Coppen A. Lithium in unipolar depression and the prevention of suicide. *The Journal of Clinical Psychiatry*. 2000;61 (Suppl 9):52-6.

[56] Rutz W, Knorring Lv, Wålinder J. Long-term effects of an educational program for general practitioners given by the Swedish Committee for

the Prevention and Treatment of Depression. *Acta Psychiatrica Scandinavica.* 1992;85(1):83-8.

[57] Hampton T. Depression care effort brings dramatic drop in large hmo population's suicide rate. *JAMA.* 2010;303(19):1903-5.

[58] Hirschfeld RB, CL, Gitlin, MJ, et al., editors. Hirschfeld R, Bowden CL, Gitlin MJ, Keck PE, Perlis RH, Suppes T, Thase ME, Wagner KD, Practice guideline for the treatment of patients with bipolar disorder (revision). *The American Journal of Psychiatry.* 2002;159(4):4-50. PubMed PMID: 220466065; 11958165.

[59] Tondo L, Isacsson G, Baldessarini R. Suicidal behaviour in bipolar disorder: Risk and prevention. *CNS drugs.* 2003;17(7):491-511.

[60] Merikangas Kr AHSAJ, et al. LIfetime and 12-month prevalence of bipolar spectrum disorder in the national comorbidity survey replication. *Archives of General Psychiatry.* 2007; 64(5):543-52.

[61] Merikangas Kr JRHJ, et al. PRevalence and correlates of bipolar spectrum disorder in the world mental health survey initiative. *Archives of General Psychiatry.* 2011; 68(3): 241-51.

[62] Allen MH, Chessick CA, Miklowitz DJ, Goldberg JF, Wisniewski SR, Miyahara S, et al. Contributors to Suicidal Ideation Among Bipolar Patients With and Without a History of Suicide Attempts. *Suicide and Life-Threatening Behavior.* 2005; 35(6): 671-80.

[63] Goodwin FK JK. *Manic-depressive illness: Bipolar disorders and recurrent depression.* 2 ed. New York: Oxford University Press; 2007.

[64] Rihmer Z, Kiss K. Bipolar disorders and suicidal behaviour. *Bipolar Disorders.* 2002; 4:21-5.

[65] Brown GK, Beck, A. T., Steer, R. A. et al. Risk factors for suicide in psychiatric outpatients: A 20-year prospective study. *Journal of Consulting and Clinical Psychology.* 2000;68(3):371–7.

[66] Rihmer Z. Prediction and prevention of suicide in bipolar disorders. *Clinical Neuropsychiatry.* 2005;2:48-54.

[67] Hawton K, Sutton, L., Haw, C., Sinclair, J. and Harriss, L. Suicide and Attempted Suicide in Bipolar Disorder: A Systematic Review of Risk Factors. *J. Clin. Psychiatry* 2005; 66:693-704.

[68] Carta M, Angst J. Epidemiological and clinical aspects of bipolar disorders: Controversies or a common need to redefine the aims and methodological aspects of surveys. *Clinical Practice and Epidemiology in Mental Health.* 2005;1(1):4.

[69] Isometsä E. Suicide in Bipolar I Disorder in Finland: Psychological Autopsy Findings from the National Suicide Prevention Project in Finland. *Archives of Suicide Research*. 2005; 9(3):251-60.
[70] Simon GE, Hunkeler E, Fireman B, Lee JY, Savarino J. Risk of suicide attempt and suicide death in patients treated for bipolar disorder. *Bipolar disorders*. 2007; 9(5): 526-30.
[71] Sharma R, Markar HR. Mortality in affective disorder. *Journal of Affective Disorders*. 1994;31(2):91-6.
[72] McIntyre RS MD, Kemp DE, Blank D, Woldeyohannes HO, Lofchy J, et al. Bipolar disorder and suicide: Research synthesis and clinical translation. *Current Psychiatry Reports*. 2008;10:66-72.
[73] Tidemalm D, Långström, N., Lichtenstein, P., Runeson, B. Risk of suicide after suicide attempt according to coexisting psychiatric disorder: Swedish cohort study with long term follow-up. *BMJ*. 2008;337:2205.
[74] Dilsaver SC CY, Swann AC, Shoaib AM, Krajewski KJ. Suicidality in patients with pure and depressive mania. *The American Journal of Psychiatry* 1994;151(9):1312-5.
[75] Righini NC, Narring F, Navarro C, Perret-Catipovic M, Ladame F, Jeannin A, et al. Antecedents, psychiatric characteristics and follow-up of adolescents hospitalized for suicide attempt of overwhelming suicidal ideation. *Swiss medical weekly*. 2005; 135(29-30):440-7.
[76] Valtonen HM, Suominen K, Haukka J, Mantere O, Leppämäki S, Arvilommi P, et al. Differences in incidence of suicide attempts during phases of bipolar I and II disorders. *Bipolar Disorders*. 2008;10(5):588-96.
[77] Pompili M, Rihmer Z, Innamorati M, Lester D, Girardi P, Tatarelli R. Assessment and treatment of suicide risk in bipolar disorders. *Expert review of neurotherapeutics*. 2009; 9(1):109-36.
[78] Valtonen HM, Suominen K, Mantere O, Leppämäki S, Arvilommi P, Isometsä E. Suicidal behaviour during different phases of bipolar disorder. *Journal of Affective Disorders*. 2007; 97(1–3):101-7.
[79] Dunner Dl FRR. CLinical factors in lithium carbonate prophylaxis failure. *Archives of General Psychiatry*. 1974;30(2):229-33.
[80] Gao K, Tolliver, BK., Kemp, DE., Ganocy, SJ., Bilali, S., Brady, KL., Findling, RL., and Calabrese, JR. Correlates of Historical Suicide Attempt in Rapid-Cycling Bipolar Disorder: A Cross-Sectional Assessment. *J. Clin. Psychiatry* 2009;70(7):1032-40.
[81] Schneck CD, Miklowitz DJ, Calabrese JR, Allen MH, et al. Phenomenology of Rapid-Cycling Bipolar Disorder: Data From the First

500 Participants in the Systematic Treatment Enhancement Program. *The American Journal of Psychiatry*. 2004; 161(10): 1902-8.
[82] Garcia-Amador M, Colom F, Valenti M, Horga G, Vieta E. Suicide risk in rapid cycling bipolar patients. *Journal of Affective Disorders*. 2009;117(1–2):74-8.
[83] Coryell W SD, Turvey C, Keller M, Leon AC, Endicott J, Schettler P, Judd L, Mueller T. The long-term course of rapid-cycling bipolar disorder. *Archives of General Psychiatry*. 2003;60(9):914-20.
[84] Angst J, Gamma, A. and Lewinsohn, P. The evolving epidemiology of bipolar disorder. *World Psychiatry*. 2002;1(3):146-8.
[85] Leverich GS, Altshuler L., Frye, MA, Suppes T, Keck P, MacElroy, S, Denicoff K, Obrocea G, Nolen W., Kupka R., Walden J., Grunze H., Perez S., Luckenbaugh D. and Post R. Factors Associated With Suicide Attempts in 648 Patients With Bipolar Disorder in the Stanley Foundation Bipolar Network. *J. Clin. Psychiatry*. 2003;64(5):506-15.
[86] Marangell LB, Bauer MS, Dennehy EB, Wisniewski SR, Allen MH, Miklowitz DJ, et al. Prospective predictors of suicide and suicide attempts in 1,556 patients with bipolar disorders followed for up to 2 years. *Bipolar disorders*. 2006;8(5 pt 2):566-75.
[87] Rihmer Z. Pharmacological prevention of suicide in bipolar patients — A realizable target. *Journal of Affective Disorders*. 2007;103(1–3):1-3.
[88] McElroy SL AL, Suppes T, Keck PE Jr, Frye MA, Denicoff KD, Nolen WA, Kupka RW, Leverich GS, Rochussen JR, Rush AJ, Post RM. Axis I psychiatric comorbidity and its relationship to historical illness variables in 288 patients with bipolar disorder. *The American Journal of Psychiatry*. 2001;158(3):420-6.
[89] Cheng A, Mann, AH., Chan, KA. Personality disorder and suicide: A case-control study. *The British Journal of Psychiatry*. 1997;170: 441-6.
[90] Foster T, Gillespie, K., McClelland, R., Patterson, C. Risk factors for suicide independent of DSM-III-R axis I disorder - Case-control psychological autopsy study in Northern Ireland. *British Journal of Psychiatry*. 1999;175:175-9.
[91] Hawton K, Houston K, Haw C, Townsend E, Harriss L. Comorbidity of axis I and axis II disorders in patients who attempted suicide. *The American Journal of Psychiatry*. 2003; 160(8):1494-500.
[92] Hawton K, Hall S, Simkin S, Bale L, Bond A, Codd S, et al. Deliberate self-harm in adolescents: A study of characteristics and trends in Oxford, 1990-2000. *Journal of child psychology and psychiatry, and allied disciplines*. 2003;44(8):1191-8.

[93] Kessler R, Borges, G., Walters, EE. Prevalence of and risk factors for lifetime suicide attempts in the National Comorbidity Survey. *Archives of General Psychiatry* 1999; 56:617–26.
[94] Nock MK, Borges G, Bromet EJ, Cha CB, Kessler RC, Lee S. Suicide and Suicidal Behavior. *Epidemiologic reviews*. 2008;30(1):133-54.
[95] Baldessarini R, Tondo, L., Hennen, J. Treatment Delays in Bipolar Disorders. *The American Journal of Psychiatry*. 1999;156(5):811-2.
[96] Chen Y-W, Dilsaver, Steven C. Lifetime rates of suicide attempts among subjects with bipolar and unipolar disorders relative to subjects with other axis I disorders. *Biological Psychiatry*. 1996;39(10):896-9.
[97] World Health Organization. *World Suicide Prevention Day* 2012 2012 [cited 2012 December 15]. Available from: http://www.emro.who.int /media/news/suicide-prevention-day2012.html.
[98] Burrows S, Auger N, Roy M, Alix C. Socio-economic inequalities in suicide attempts and suicide mortality in Québec, Canada, 1990–2005. *Public health*. 2010; 124(2): 78-85.
[99] Denney JT, Rogers RG, Krueger PM, Wadsworth T. Adult Suicide Mortality in the United States: Marital Status, Family Size, Socioeconomic Status, and Differences by Sex. *Social Science Quarterly*. 2009;90(5):1167-85.
[100] Biddle L, Brock A, Brookes ST, Gunnell D. Suicide rates in young men in England and Wales in the 21st century: Time trend study. *BMJ*. 2008; 336(7643):539-42.
[101] McPhedran S, Baker J. Recent Australian suicide trends for males and females at the national level: Has the rate of decline differed? *Health Policy*. 2008;87(3):350-8.
[102] Borges G, Orozco, R., Benjet, C., Medina-Mora, M. E. Suicidio y conductas suicidas en México: Retrospectiva y situación actual. *Salud Pública de México*. 2010; 52: 292-304.
[103] Chang S-S, Gunnell D, Sterne JAC, Lu T-H, Cheng ATA. Was the economic crisis 1997–1998 responsible for rising suicide rates in East/Southeast Asia? A time–trend analysis for Japan, Hong Kong, South Korea, Taiwan, Singapore and Thailand. *Social science and medicine*. 2009;68(7):1322-31.
[104] Thomas K, Gunnell D. Suicide in England and Wales 1861–2007: A time-trends analysis. *International Journal of epidemiology*. 2010;39(6):1464-75.
[105] World health Organization. *How can suicide be prevented?* 2012 [cited 2012 December 15]. Available from: http://www.who.int/features/qa/24.

[106] Catalano R, Goldman-Mellor S, Saxton K, Margerison-Zilko C, Subbaraman M, LeWinn K, et al. The Health Effects of Economic Decline. *Annual Review of Public Health*. 2011;32(1):431-50.

[107] Suzuki T. Economic modelling of suicide under income uncertainty: For better understanding of middle-aged suicide. *Australian Economic Papers*. 2008; 47(3): 296-310.

[108] Gutiérrez-García AG C, CM, Orozco R, El suicidio, conceptos actuales. *Salud Mental*. 2006;29:66-74.

[109] Bertolote J, Fleishman, A. A global perspective in the epidemiology of suicide. *Suicidology*. 2002;7:6-8.

[110] Durkheim E. *Suicide: A Study in Sociology*. Free Press: New York.1951.

[111] Yamamura E. The different impacts of socioeconomic factors on suicide between males and females. *Applied Economics Letters*. 2010;17:1009-12.

[112] Zivin K, Paczkowski M, Galea S. Economic downturns and population mental health: Research findings, gaps, challenges and priorities. *Psychological medicine*. 2011; 41(07): 1343.

[113] Chen Y, Yip, PSF., Lee, C., Fan, H., Fu, K. Economic fluctuations and suicide: A comparison of Taiwan and Hong Kong. *Social Science and Medicine*. 2010;71:2083-90.

[114] Stiglitz JE. Empleo, justicia social y bienestar de la sociedad. *Revista Internacional del Trabajo*. 2002;121(1-2):9-31.

[115] Gunnell D, Wheeler B, Chang SS, Thomas B, Sterne JAC, Dorling D. Changes in the geography of suicide in young men: England and Wales 1981–2005. *Journal of epidemiology and community health*. 2010; 66(6): 536-43.

[116] World Health Organization. *Impact of economic crises on mental health* 2007 [cited 2011 March 21]. Available from: http://www.euro.who.int /data/assets/pdf_file/0008/ 134999/e94837.pdf.

[117] Kuroki M. Suicide and unemployment in Japan: Evidence from municipal level suicide rates and age-specific suicide rates. *Journal of Socio-economics*. 2010;39(6):683-91.

[118] Tapia Granados JA, Ionides EL. Mortality and Macroeconomic Fluctuations in Contemporary Sweden. *European Journal of Population*. 2011; 27(2):157-84.

[119] Rahman T, Mittelhammer RC, Wandschneider PR. Measuring quality of life across countries: A multiple indicators and multiple causes approach. *Journal of Socio-economics*. 2011;40(1):43-52.

[120] Ferretti F, Coluccia A. Socio-economic factors and suicide rates in European Union countries. *Legal Medicine*. 2009;11(Suppl 1):S92-S4.

[121] Economou M, Madianos M, Peppou LE, Patelakis A, Stefanis CN. Major depression in the Era of economic crisis: A replication of a cross-sectional study across Greece. *Journal of Affective Disorders*. 2013; 145(3): 308-14.

[122] Economou M, Madianos M, Theleritis C, Peppou LE, Stefanis CN. Increased suicidality amid economic crisis in Greece. *The Lancet*. 2011; 378(9801):1459.

[123] Borowy I. *Crisis as opportunity: International health work during the economic depression* 2008.

[124] Gilchrist H, Howarth G, Sullivan G. The Cultural Context of Youth Suicide in Australia: Unemployment, Identity and Gender. *Social Policy and Society*. 2007; 6(2):151.

[125] Mandal B, Roe, B. Job loss, retirement and mental health of older Americans. *The Journal of Mental Health Policy and Economics*. 2008;11:167-76.

[126] Stuckler D, Basu S, Suhrcke M, Coutts A, McKee M. The public health effect of economic crises and alternative policy responses in Europe: An empirical analysis. *The Lancet*. 2009;374(9686):315-23.

[127] Lee S, Guo W-j, Tsang A, Mak ADP, Wu J, Ng KL, et al. Evidence for the 2008 economic crisis exacerbating depression in Hong Kong. *Journal of Affective Disorders*. 2010; 126(1–2):125-33.

[128] Inoue K, Nishimura Y, Nishida A, Fukunaga T, Masaki M, Fujita Y, et al. Relationships between suicide and three economic factors in South Korea. *Legal Medicine*. 2010;12(2):100-1.

[129] Khan S, Murray RP, Barnes GE. A structural equation model of the effect of poverty and unemployment on alcohol abuse. *Addictive Behaviors*. 2002;27(3):405-23.

[130] Gunnell D, Platt S, Hawton K. The economic crisis and suicide. *BMJ*. 2009; 338:1891.

[131] Hulten A, Jiang GX, Wasserman D, Hawton K, Hjelmeland H, De Leo D, et al. Repetition of attempted suicide among teenagers in Europe: Frequency, timing and risk factors. *European child and adolescent psychiatry*. 2001;10(3):161-9.

[132] Miranda R, Scott M, Hicks R, Wilcox HC, Harris Munfakh JL, Shaffer D. Suicide Attempt Characteristics, Diagnoses, and Future Attempts: Comparing Multiple Attempters to Single Attempters and Ideators.

Journal of the American Academy of Child and Adolescent Psychiatry. 2008; 47(1):32-40.

[133] Ruengorn C, Sanichwankul, K., Niwatananum, W., Mahatnirunkul, S., Pumpaisalchai, W., Patumanond, J. Incidence and risk factors of suicide reattempts within 1 year after psychiatric hospital discharge in mood disorder patients. *Clinical Epidemiology.* 2011; 3:305–13.

[134] Scoliers G, Portzky G, van Heeringen K, Audenaert K. Sociodemographic and psychopathological risk factors for repetition of attempted suicide: A 5-year follow-up study. *Archives of suicide research: Official Journal of the International Academy for Suicide Research.* 2009;13(3):201-13.

[135] Brådvik L, Berglund, M. Repetition of suicide attempts across episodes of severe depression: Behavioural sensitisation found in suicide group but not in controls. *BMC Psychiatry.* 2011;11(1):5.

[136] Leon AC, Friedman RA, Sweeney JA, Brown RP, Mann JJ. Statistical issues in the identification of risk factors for suicidal behavior: The application of survival analysis. *Psychiatry research.* 1990;31(1):99-108.

[137] Trémeau F, Staner L, Duval F, Corrêa H, Crocq M-A, Darreye A, et al. Suicide attempts and family history of suicide in three psychiatric populations. *Suicide and Life-Threatening Behavior.* 2005;35(6):702-13.

[138] Spirito A, Plummer B, Gispert M, Levy S, Kurkjian J, Lewander W, et al. Adolescent suicide attempts: Outcomes at Follow-Up. *American Journal of Orthopsychiatry.* 1992;62(3):464-8.

[139] Cedereke M, Ojehagen A. Prediction of repeated parasuicide after 1-12 months. *European psychiatry: The Journal of the Association of European Psychiatrists.* 2005;20(2):101-9.

[140] Colman I, Newman SC, Schopflocher D, Bland RC, Dyck RJ. A multivariate study of predictors of repeat parasuicide. *Acta Psychiatrica Scandinavica.* 2004; 109(4): 306-12.

[141] Kapur N, Cooper J, King-Hele S, Webb R, Lawlor M, Rodway C, et al. The repetition of suicidal behavior: A multicenter cohort study. *Journal of Clinical Psychiatry.* 2006;67(10):1599-609.

[142] Christiansen E, Jensen BF. Risk of repetition of suicide attempt, suicide or all deaths after an episode of attempted suicide: A register-based survival analysis. *The Australian and New Zealand Journal of Psychiatry.* 2007;41(3):257-65.

[143] Groholt B, Ekeberg O, Haldorsen T. Adolescent suicide attempters: What predicts future suicidal acts? *Suicide and life-threatening behavior.* 2006; 36(6):638-50.

[144] Haukka J, Suominen K, Partonen T, Lonnqvist J. Determinants and outcomes of serious attempted suicide: A nationwide study in Finland, 1996-2003. *American Journal of Epidemiology.* 2008;167(10):1155-63.

[145] Dieserud G, Røysamb E, Braverman MT, Dalgard OS, Ekeberg Ø. Predicating repetition of suicide attempt: A prospective study of 50 suicide attempters. *Archives of Suicide Research.* 2003;7(1):1-15.

[146] Lopez-Castroman J, Perez-Rodriguez Mde L, Jaussent I, Alegria AA, Artes-Rodriguez A, Freed P, et al. Distinguishing the relevant features of frequent suicide attempters. *Journal of psychiatric research.* 2011; 45(5): 619-25.

[147] Bryan CJ, Johnson LG, David Rudd M, Joiner TE. Hypomanic symptoms among first-time suicide attempters predict future multiple attempt status. *Journal of clinical psychology.* 2008;64(4):519-30.

[148] Jeglic EL, Sharp IR, Chapman JE, Brown GK, Beck AT. History of Family Suicide Behaviors and Negative Problem Solving in Multiple Suicide Attempters. *Archives of Suicide Research.* 2005;9(2):135-46.

[149] Monnin J, Thiemard E, Vandel P, Nicolier M, Tio G, Courtet P, et al. Sociodemographic and psychopathological risk factors in repeated suicide attempts: Gender differences in a prospective study. *Journal of affective disorders.* 2012; 136 (1-2): 35-43.

[150] Andover MS, Zlotnick C, Miller IW. Childhood physical and sexual abuse in depressed patients with single and multiple suicide attempts. *Suicide and life-threatening behavior.* 2007;37(4):467-74.

[151] Ystgaard M, Hestetun I, Loeb M, Mehlum L. Is there a specific relationship between childhood sexual and physical abuse and repeated suicidal behavior? *Child abuse and neglect.* 2004;28(8):863-75.

[152] McAuliffe C, Keeley HS, Corcoran P. Problem solving and repetition of parasuicide. *Behavioural and Cognitive Psychotherapy.* 2002;30(4):385-97.

[153] Pompili M, Innamorati M, Szanto K, Di Vittorio C, Conwell Y, Lester D, et al. Life events as precipitants of suicide attempts among first-time suicide attempters, repeaters, and non-attempters. *Psychiatry research.* 2011;186(2-3):300-5.

[154] Aghanwa H. The determinants of attempted suicide in a general hospital setting in Fiji Islands: A gender-specific study. *General hospital psychiatry.* 2004;26(1):63-9.

[155] Värnik A, Kõlves K, Allik J, Arensman E, Aromaa E, van Audenhove C, et al. Gender issues in suicide rates, trends and methods among youths aged 15–24 in 15 European countries. *Journal of affective disorders.* 2009; 113(3):216-26.
[156] Canetto SS, Sakinofsky I. The gender paradox in suicide. *Suicide and Life - Threatening Behavior.* 1998;28(1):1-23.
[157] Carroll-Ghosh T, Victor, B.S., Bourgeois, J.A. Suicide. In: Hales RE, Yodofsky, S.C., editor. *The American Psychiatric Publishing Textbok of Clinical Psychiatry.* Washington D.C: American Psychiatric Publishing, Inc.; 2003.
[158] Sudak H. Suicide. In: Sadock BJ, Sadock, C.V.A. (Eds.), editor. *Kaplan and Sadock's Comprehensive Textbook of Psychiatry.* 8th Edition ed. Philadelphia: Lippincott Williams and Wilkins; 2005.
[159] Phillips MR, Cheng HG. The changing global face of suicide. *The Lancet.* 2012; 379(9834): 2318-9.
[160] Soman C, Safraj S, Kutty V, Vijayakumar K, Ajayan K. Suicide in South India: A community-based study in Kerala. *Indian Journal of Psychiatry.* 2009;51(4):261-4.
[161] Sudhir Kumar CT, Mohan R, Ranjith G, Chandrasekaran R. Gender differences in medically serious suicide attempts: A study from South India. *Psychiatry research.* 2006; 144(1):79-86.
[162] Kumar V. Burnt wives—a study of suicides. *Burns.* 2003;29(1):31-5.
[163] Yip PSF, Liu KY. The ecological fallacy and the gender ratio of suicide in China. *The British Journal of Psychiatry.* 2006;189(5):465-6.
[164] Women and Suicidal Behavior: A Cultural Analysis. *American Journal of Orthopsychiatry.* 2008;78(2):259-66.
[165] Brent DA, Baugher M, Bridge J, Chen T, Chiappetta L. Age- and Sex-Related Risk Factors for Adolescent Suicide. *Journal of the American Academy of Child and Adolescent Psychiatry.* 1999;38(12):1497-505.
[166] Gonda X, Pompili M, Serafini G, Montebovi F, Campi S, Dome P, et al. Suicidal behavior in bipolar disorder: Epidemiology, characteristics and major risk factors. *Journal of Affective Disorders.* 2012;143(1–3):16-26.
[167] Zalsman G, Braun M, Arendt M, Grunebaum MF, Sher L, Burke AK, et al. A comparison of the medical lethality of suicide attempts in bipolar and major depressive disorders. *Bipolar Disorders.* 2006;8(5p2):558-65.
[168] Kwon J-W, Chun H, Cho S-i. A closer look at the increase in suicide rates in South Korea from 1986-2005. *BMC Public Health.* 2009; 9(1):72.

[169] American Foundation for suicide prevention (AFSP). *Facts and Figures about Suicide 1998* [cited 2011 November 21]. Available from: www.afsp.org.
[170] Dervic K, Brent DA, Oquendo MA. Completed Suicide in Childhood. *Suicidal Behavior: A Developmental Perspective.* 2008;31(2):271-91.
[171] Groholt B, Ekeberg, O., Wichstrom, L., Haldorssen, T. Suicide among children and younger and older adolescents in Norway: A comparative study. *Journal of the American Academy of Child and Adolescent Psychiatry.* 1998;37:473-81.
[172] Karch D, Logan, J., McDaniel, D., Parks, Sh., Patel, N. Surveillance for Violent Deaths — National Violent Death Reporting System, 16 States, 2009. *Morbidity and Mortality Weekly Report (MMWR)* [Internet]. 2012; 61(6):[1-43 pp.]. Available from: http://www.cdc.gov/mmwr/preview/ mmwrhtml/ss6106a1.htm.
[173] Blum RW, Nelson-Mmari K. The health of young people in a global context. *Journal of Adolescent Health.* 2004;35(5):402-18.
[174] Sørensen MJ, Nissen JB, Mors O, Thomsen PH. Age and gender differences in depressive symptomatology and comorbidity: An incident sample of psychiatrically admitted children. *Journal of Affective Disorders.* 2005;84(1):85-91.
[175] Essau CA, Lewinsohn PM, Seeley JR, Sasagawa S. Gender differences in the developmental course of depression. *Journal of Affective Disorders.* 2010; 127 (1–3):185-90.
[176] Essau CA, Rer S, Conradt J, Petermann F, Phil. Frequency, Comorbidity, and Psychosocial Impairment of Anxiety Disorders in German Adolescents. *Journal of Anxiety Disorders.* 2000;14(3):263-79.
[177] Baca-garcia E, Perez-rodriguez MM, Keyes KM, Oquendo MA, Hasin DS, Grant BF, et al. Suicidal ideation and suicide attempts in the United States: 1991-1992 and 2001-2002. *Molecular psychiatry.* 2010; 15(3): 250-9.
[178] Eaton D, Kann, L., Kinchen, S., Shanklin, S., Ross, J. et al. Youth Risk Behavior Surveillance --- United States, 2007. *MMWR Surveillance Summary.* 2008;57(4):1-131.
[179] Eaton DK, Kann L, Kinchen S, Ross J, Hawkins J, Harris WA, et al. Youth Risk Behavior Surveillance?United States, 2005. *Journal of School Health.* 2006; 76(7): 353-72.
[180] Grunbaum J, Kann, L., Kinchen, S., Ross, J., Hawkins, J., Lowry, R., et al. Youth risk behavior surveillance—United States, 2003. *MMWR Surveillance Summary.* 2004; 53(2):1-96.

[181] Saunders KEA, Hawton K. Suicidal behaviour and the menstrual cycle. *Psychological medicine.* 2006;36(7):901.

[182] Levinson D, Haklai Z, Stein N, Ethel-Sherry G. Suicide Attempts in Israel: Age by Gender Analysis of a National Emergency Departments Database. *Suicide and Life - Threatening Behavior.* 2006;36(1):97-102.

[183] Shaffer D, Garland ANN, Gould M, Fisher P, Trautman P. Preventing Teenage Suicide: A Critical Review. *Journal of the American Academy of Child and Adolescent Psychiatry.* 1988;27(6):675-87.

[184] Lewinsohn PM, Rohde P, Seeley JR, Baldwin CL. Gender Differences in Suicide Attempts From Adolescence to Young Adulthood. *Journal of the American Academy of Child and Adolescent Psychiatry.* 2001;40(4): 427-34.

[185] Black DW, Blum N, Pfohl B, Hale N. Suicidal behavior in borderline personality disorder: Prevalence, risk factors, prediction, and prevention. *Journal of personality disorders.* 2004;18(3):226-39.

[186] Patton GC, Coffey C, Sawyer SM, Viner RM, Haller DM, Bose K, et al. Global patterns of mortality in young people: A systematic analysis of population health data. *The Lancet.* 2009;374(9693):881-92.

[187] Koo J, Cox WM. An economic interpretation of suicide cycles in Japan. *Contemporary Economic Policy.* 2008;26(1):162-74.

[188] Page A, Morrell S, Taylor R. Suicide differentials in Australian males and females by various measures of socio-economic status, 1994-98. *Australian and New Zealand Journal of Public Health.* 2002;26(4):318-24.

[189] Cutright P, Stack S, Fernquist R. Marital Status Integration, Suicide Disapproval, and Societal Integration as Explanations of Marital Status Differences in Female Age-Specific Suicide Rates. *Suicide and Life - Threatening Behavior.* 2007;37(6):715-24.

[190] Minoiu C, Andrés AR. The effect of public spending on suicide: Evidence from U.S. state data. *Journal of Socio-economics.* 2008; 37(1): 237-61.

[191] Kposowa AJ. Marital status and suicide in the national longitudinal mortality study. *Journal of epidemiology and community health.* 2000; 54(4):254-61.

[192] World health Organization. European mortality database (MDB). *World Health Organization Regional Office for Europe* 2012 [cited 2012 December 11]. Available from: http://data.euro.who.int/hfamdb.

[193] National Center for Injury Prevention and Control. *WISQARS Fatal Injury Reports, National and Regional,* 1999 - 2010 2012 [cited 2012

September 21]. Available from: http://webappa.cdc.gov/sasweb/ncipc/mortrate10_us.html.

[194] De Leo D, Padoani W, Scocco P, Lie D, Bille-Brahe U, Arensman E, et al. Attempted and completed suicide in older subjects: Results from the WHO/EURO Multicentre Study of Suicidal Behaviour. *International Journal of geriatric psychiatry*. 2001;16(3):300-10.

[195] Klein S, Christoph Bischoff, Ch., Schweitzerb, W. Suicides in the Canton of Zurich (Switzerland). *Swiss Med. Wkly*. 2010;140:w13102.

[196] Karch D. Sex Differences in Suicide Incident Characteristics and Circumstances among Older Adults: Surveillance Data from the National Violent Death Reporting System-17 U.S. States, 2007-2009. *International Journal of Environmental Research and Public Health*. 2011; 8(8):3479-95.

[197] Carney S, Rich, CL., Burke, PA., et al. Suicide over 60: The San Diego Study. *Journal of the American Geriatric Society*. 1994;42:174–80.

[198] Wanta B, Schlotthauer, AE., Guse, CE. et al. The burden of suicide in Wisconsin's older adult population. *WMJ*. 2009;108(2):87-93.

[199] Shah A. The relationship between suicide rates and age: An analysis of multinational data from the World Health Organization. *International Psychogeriatrics*. 2007; 19(06): 1141.

[200] Appleby L, Mortensen PB, Faragher EB. Suicide and other causes of mortality after post-partum psychiatric admission. *The British Journal of Psychiatry*. 1998; 173(3): 209-11.

[201] Lindahl V, Pearson JL, Colpe L. Prevalence of suicidality during pregnancy and the postpartum. *Archives of Women's Mental Health*. 2005; 8(2):77-87.

[202] Henshaw C. Maternal Suicide. In: Cockburn J, Pawson M, editors. *Psychological Challenges in Obstetrics and Gynecology*: Springer London; 2007. p. 157-64.

[203] Gissler M, Hemminki E, Lonnqvist J. Suicides after pregnancy in Finland, 1987-94: Register linkage study. *British Medical Journal*. 1996; 313(7070): 1431.

[204] Andersson L, Sundström-Poromaa I, Bixo M, Wulff M, Bondestam K, Åström M. Point prevalence of psychiatric disorders during the second trimester of pregnancy: A population-based study. *American Journal of Obstetrics and Gynecology*. 2003;189(1):148-54.

[205] Melville JL, Gavin AMSW, Guo YMSN, Fan M, Katon WJ. Depressive Disorders During Pregnancy: Prevalence and Risk Factors in a Large Urban Sample. *Obstetrics and Gynecology*. 2010;116(5):1064-70.

[206] da Silva R, da Costa Ores L, Jansen K, da Silva Moraes I, de Mattos Souza L, Magalhães P, et al. *Suicidality and Associated Factors in Pregnant Women in Brazil.* Springer Netherlands; 2012. p. 392-5.

[207] Reck C, Struben K, Backenstrass M, Stefenelli U, Reinig K, Fuchs T, et al. Prevalence, onset and comorbidity of postpartum anxiety and depressive disorders. *Acta Psychiatrica Scandinavica.* 2008;118(6):459-68.

[208] Frautschi S, Cerulli A, Maine D. Suicide during pregnancy and its neglect as a component of maternal mortality. *International Journal of Gynecology and Obstetrics.* 1994; 47(3):275-84.

[209] Lewinsohn PM, Hops H, Roberts RE, Seeley JR, Andrews JA. Adolescent psychopathology: I. Prevalence and incidence of depression and other DSM-III—R disorders in high school students. *Journal of abnormal psychology.*1993;102(1):133-44.

[210] Schoenbach B, Garrison, C., Kaplan, B. Epidemiology of adolescent depression. *Public Health Review.* 1984;12:159-89.

[211] Gunnell D, Middleton N, Whitley E, Dorling D, Frankel S. Why are suicide rates rising in young men but falling in the elderly?—a time-series analysis of trends in England and Wales 1950–1998. *Social science and medicine.* 2003;57(4):595-611.

[212] Kuroki M. Suicide and unemployment in Japan: Evidence from municipal level suicide rates and age-specific suicide rates. *The Journal of Socio-Economics.* 2010; 39(6): 683-91.

[213] Usall J, Pinto-Meza A, Fernández A, Graaf Rd, Demyttenaere K, Alonso J, et al. Suicide ideation across reproductive life cycle of women Results from a European epidemiological study. *Journal of affective disorders.* 2009; 116(1–2):144-7.

[214] Knox K, Conwell, Y., Caine ED. If suicide is a public health problem, what are we doing to prevent it? *American Journal of Public Health.* 2004; 94(1):37-45.

[215] World Health Organization. *Mental health: Strengthening our response* 2010 [cited 2012 July 19]. Available from: http://www.who.int /mediacentre/factsheets/fs220/en/ index.html.

[216] Hawton K, Harriss, L., Zahl, D. Deaths from all causes in a long-term follow-up study of 11,583 deliberate self-harmpatients. *Psychol. Med.* 2006;36:397-405.

[217] Luoma J, Martin, CE., Pearson, JL. Contact with mental health and primary care providers before suicide: A reviewof the evidence. *The American Journal of Psychiatry.* 2002;159:909-16.

[218] Andersen U, Andersen, M., Rosholm, JU., Gram, LF. Contacts to the health care system prior to suicide: A comprehensive analysis using registers for general and psychiatric hospital admissions, contacts to general practitioners andpracticing specialists and drugprescriptions. *Acta Psychiatrica Scandinavica* 2000; 102:126-34.
[219] Cassidy F. Risk Factors of Attempted Suicide in Bipolar Disorder. *Suicide and Life - Threatening Behavior*. 2011;41(1):6.
[220] Mann JJ, Apter A, Bertolote J, Beautrais A, Currier D, Haas A, et al. Suicide prevention strategies: A systematic review. *JAMA: The journal of the American Medical Association*. 2005; 294(16):2064-74.
[221] Linehan MM CK, Murray AM, Brown MZ, Gallop RJ, Heard HL, Korslund KE, Tutek DA, Reynolds SK, Lindenboim N. Two-year randomized controlled trial and follow-up of dialectical behavior therapy vs therapy by experts for suicidal behaviors and borderline personality disorder. *Archives of General Psychiatry*. 2006;63(7):757-66.
[222] Evans DJ, Pillay AL. Mental health problems of men attending district-level clinical psychology services in South Africa. *Psychological reports*. 2009;104(3):773-83.
[223] Bateman A, Fonagy, P., Effectiveness of Partial Hospitalization in the Treatment of Borderline Personality Disorder: A Randomized Controlled Trial. *The American Journal of Psychiatry* 1999;156:1563-9.
[224] McAuliffe C, Corcoran P, Hickey P, McLeavey BC. Optional thinking ability among hospital-treated deliberate self-harm patients: A 1-year follow-up study. *The British Journal of clinical psychology / the British Psychological Society*. 2008; 47 (Pt 1): 43-58.
[225] Guthrie E, Kapur N, Mackway-Jones K, Chew-Graham C, Moorey J, Mendel E, et al. Randomised controlled trial of brief psychological intervention after deliberate self poisoning. *BMJ* (Clinical research ed). 2001;323(7305):135-8.
[226] Harrington R, Kerfoot, M., Dyer, E., McNiven, F., Gill, J., Harrington, V., Woodham, A. Deliberate self-poisoning in adolescence: Why does a brief family intervention work in some cases and not others? *Journal of Adolescence*. 2000;23(1):13-20.
[227] Bergmans Y, Langley J, Links P, Lavery JV. The Perspectives of Young Adults on Recovery from Repeated Suicide-Related Behavior. Crisis: *The Journal of Crisis Intervention and Suicide Prevention*. 2009; 30(3): 120-7.
[228] Bergmans Y, Links PS. A description of a psychosocial/ psycho-educational intervention for persons with recurrent suicide attempts.

Crisis: The Journal of Crisis Intervention and Suicide Prevention. 2002;23(4):156-60.

[229] Evans M, Morgan, HG., Hayward, A., Gunnell, DJ. Crisis telephone consultation for deliberate self-harm patients: Effects on repetition. *British Journal of Psychiatry.* 1999; 175:23-7.

[230] Bertolote JM, Fleischmann A, De Leo D, Phillips MR, Botega NJ, Vijayakumar L, et al. Repetition of suicide attempts: Data from emergency care settings in five culturally different low- and middle-income countries participating in the WHO SUPRE-MISS Study. *Crisis.* 2010; 31(4):194-201.

[231] Hvid M, Wang AG. Preventing repetition of attempted suicide--I. Feasibility (acceptability, adherence, and effectiveness) of a Baerum-model like aftercare. *Nordic Journal of psychiatry.* 2009;63(2):148-53.

[232] Evans J, Evans, M., Morgan, HG., Hayward, A., Gunnell, D. Crisis card following self-harm: 12-month follow-up of a randomised controlled trial. *Br. J. Psychiatry.* 2005; 187: 186-7.

[233] Vaiva G, Walter M, Al Arab AS, Courtet P, Bellivier F, Demarty AL, et al. ALGOS: The development of a randomized controlled trial testing a case management algorithm designed to reduce suicide risk among suicide attempters. *BMC Psychiatry.* 2011;11.

[234] Motto J, Bostrom, AG. A randomized controlled trial of postcrisis suicide prevention. *Psychiatric Services.* 2001;52:828-33.

[235] Carter G, Clover, K., Whyte, IM., Dawson, AH., D'Este, C. Postcards from the EDge project: Randomised controlled trial of an intervention using postcards to reduce repetition of hospital treated deliberate self poisoning. *BMJ.* 2005;331(7520):805.

[236] Rutz W, von Knorring, L., Walinder, J. Frequency of suicide on Gotland after systematic postgraduate education of general practitioners. *Acta Psychiatrica Scandinavica.* 1989;80:151-4.

[237] Szanto K, Kalmar, S., Hendin, H., Rihmer, Z., Mann, JJ. A suicide prevention program in a region with a very high suicide rate. *Archives of General Psychiatry.* 2007; 64(8):914-20.

[238] Kerkhof AJFM. The Finnish national suicide prevention program evaluated. *Crisis: The Journal of Crisis Intervention and Suicide Prevention.* 1999;20(2):50-,63. PubMed PMID: 614464032; 2007-11363-001. English.

[239] Department of Health. *England. National suicide prevention strategy for England 2002* [cited 2012 March 29]. Available from: http://www.dh.

gov.uk/en/Publicationsandstatistics/Publications/PublicationsPolicyAnd Guidance/DH_4009474.

[240] Flemish Menatl Haelth Centres. *Suicide Prevention Program 2007* [cited 2011 November 27]. Available from: http://www.ec-mental-health-process.net/pdf/ flemish_suicide_prevention_plan._pdf.

[241] Hawton K, Harriss L, Hall S, Simkin S, Bale E, Bond A. Deliberate self-harm in Oxford, 1990-2000: A time of change in patient characteristics. *Psychological medicine*. 2003; 33(6):987-95.

[242] Gunnell D, Ashby, D. Antidepressants and suicide: What is the balance of benefit and harm. *BMJ*. 2004; 329:34-8.

[243] Martín Arias L, Lobato, C., Ortega, S., Velasco, A., Carvajal, A., García del Pozo, J. Trends in the consumption of antidepressants in Castilla y Leon (Spain). Association between suicide rates and antidepressant drug consumption. *Pharmacoepidemiology and drug safety*. 2010;19:895-900.

[244] Filteau M, Lapierre, YD., Bakish, D. et al. Reduction in suicidal ideation with SSRIs: A review of 459 depressed patients. *Journal of Psychiatry and Neuroscience*. 1993; 18(3):114-9.

[245] Kapur S, Mieczkowski, T., and Mann, JJ. Antidepressant medications and the relative risk of suicide attempt and suicide. *Journal of the American Medical Association*. 1992; 268: 3441-5.

[246] Cipriani A, Pretty, H., Hawton, K., Geddes, J. Lithium in the prevention of suicidal behaviour and all-cause mortality in patients with mood disorders: A systematic review of randomised trials. *The American Journal of Psychiatry*. 2005;162:1805-19.

[247] Goodwin RD, Kroenke K, Hoven CW, Spitzer RL. Major depression, physical illness, and suicidal ideation in primary care. *Psychosomatic medicine*. 2003;65(4):501-5.

[248] Swann A, Bowden, CL., Calabrese, JR. et al. Pattern of response to divalproex, lithium, or placebo in four naturalistic subtypes of mania. *Neuropsychopharmacology*. 2002; 26(4): 530-6.

[249] Bruce M, Ten Have, TR., Reynolds, CF III., Katz II, Schulberg, HC., Mulsant, BH., et al. Reducing suicidal ideation and depressive symptoms in depressed older primary care patients: A randomized controlled trial. *JAMA*. 2004;291:1081-91.

[250] Tiihonen J, Lonnqvist J, Wahlbeck K, Klaukka T, Tanskanen A, Haukka J. Antidepressants and the risk of suicide, attempted suicide, and overall mortality in a nationwide cohort. *Archives of General Psychiatry*. 2006; 63(12):1358-67.

[251] Saunders KaH, K. The role of psychopharmacology in suicide prevention. *Epidemiologia e Psichiatria Sociale*. 2009;18(3):172-8.

[252] Gibbons R, Hur, K., Bhaumik, DK., Mann, JJ. The relationship between antidepressant medication use and rate of suicide. *Archives of General Psychiatry*. 2005; 62(2):165-72.

[253] Healy D. Lines of evidence on the risks of suicide with selective serotonin reuptake inhibitors. *Psychotherapy and psychosomatics*. 2003; 72(2):71-9.

[254] Shah R, Uren, Z., Baker, A., Majeed, A. Deaths from antidepressants in England and Wales 1993-1997: Analysis of a new national database. *Psychol. Med.* 2001;31:1203-10.

[255] Juurlink DN, Mamdani MM, Kopp A, Redelmeier DA. The Risk of Suicide With Selective Serotonin Reuptake Inhibitors in the Elderly. *The American Journal of Psychiatry*. 2006;163(5):813-21.

[256] Whittington C, Kendall, T., Fonagy, P., et al. Selective serotonin reuptake inhibitors in childhood depression: Systematic review of published versus unpublished data. *Lancet*. 2004; 363:1341-5.

[257] Teicher M, Glod, C., Cole, JO. Emergence of intense suicidal pre-occupation during fluoxetine treatment. *The American Journal of Psychiatry*. 1990;147(207-210).

[258] Rihmer Z, Akiskal, HS. Do antidepressants t(h)reat(en) depressives? Toward a clinically judicious formulation of the antidepressant-suicidality FDA advisory in light of declining national suicide statistics from many countries. *Journal of Affective Disorders*. 2006;94:3-13.

[259] Benazzi F. Suicidal ideation and depressive mixed states. *Psychother. Psychosom.* 2005; 74:61-2.

[260] Søndergård L, Lopez AG, Andersen PK, Kessing LV. Mood-stabilizing pharmacological treatment in bipolar disorders and risk of suicide. *Bipolar Disorders*. 2008; 10(1):87-94.

[261] Kleindienst N, Greil W. Differential efficacy of lithium and carbamazepine in the prophylaxis of bipolar disorder: Results of the MAP study. *Neuropsychobiology*. 2000; 42:2-10.

[262] Guzzetta F, Tondo, L., Centorrino, F., and Baldessarini, R. *Lithium Treatment Reduces Suicide Risk in Recurrent Major Depressive Disorder*. 2007; 68(3):380-3.

[263] National Collaborating Centre for Mental Health (NCCMH). Management of depression in primary and secondary care (full guideline) *Clinical Guideline 23*. London: National Institute for Clinical Excellence; 2008.

In: Affective Disorders
Editor: Linda D. Hambrick

ISBN: 978-1-62618-402-2

Chapter 3

UNDERSTANDING THE SOCIAL IMPACT OF MAJOR AFFECTIVE DISORDERS

Gianluca Serafini**, Maurizio Pompili, Marco Innamorati, Gloria Giordano and Paolo Girardi

Department of Neurosciences, Mental Health and Sensory Organs, Suicide Prevention Center, Sant'Andrea Hospital, Rome, Italy

ABSTRACT

Mood disorders (MD) affect more than 5% of the general population determining significant functional impairment in sufferers and often leading to adverse social outcomes. MD include both the unipolar and bipolar types. Major depressive disorder is the most common affective disorder being one of the leading causes of premature death and disability among all diseases and accounting for enormous health service utilization. Comorbid anxiety and depression frequently co-exist and are associated with higher costs considering both individual and social perspectives. Patients with MD often present in primary care settings and require health care resources. Case identification and correct assessment are, no doubt, crucial in clinical practice. MD raise complicated

* Correspondence: Gianluca Serafini M.D., Ph.D., Department of Neurosciences, Mental Health and Sensory Organs – Sant'Andrea Hospital, "Sapienza" University of Rome, 1035-1039 Via di Grottarossa, 00189, Rome, Italy. Tel: +390633775675; Fax: +390633775342. E-mail: gianluca.serafini@uniroma1.it.

challenges, often leading to inadequate diagnosis and treatment resulting in unnecessary patient distress and increased utilization of health care services. Providing an effective assessment, correct evaluation, and evidence-based treatment may improve quality of life in patients with MD. We aimed to critically overview the current literature about MD, health effects, and social impact of these disabling conditions

Keywords: Major affective disorders, social impact, assessment, treatment

INTRODUCTION

Mental disorders are chronic and disabling conditions having a tremendous impact on quality of life and social functioning (Mueser et al, 1990; Murray and Lopez, 1996).

Major depressive disorders (MDD) are associated with the highest loss of productivity among all chronic conditions (Druss et al, 2000; Buist-Bouwman et al, 2005; Verow and Hargreaves, 2000; Glozier, 2002). Individuals with major depression not only suffer from higher absenteeism compared to healthy subjects but they also report lower productivity due to decreased work performance (Stewart et al, 2003; Adler et al, 2006; Kessler and Frank, 1997; Goetzel et al, 2004; Waghorn et al, 2005).

Affective symptoms may be frequently associated with severe cognitive dysfunctions (Iosifescu, 2012) which predict negative outcome and strongly affect daily activities together with social functioning (Stewart et al, 2003; Kessler and Frank, 1997; Adler et al, 2006; Lim et al, 2000; O'Neill et al, 2008; Waghorn et al, 2005).

Among MDD, several studies (Burdick et al, 2010; Judd et al, 2008) suggested that bipolar disorder (BD) has a dramatic impact on interpersonal, social, and family functioning. The World Mental Health Initiative which surveyed more than 8000 patients with BD, suggested that this illness is associated with a greater loss of disability-adjusted life years when compared with all forms of cancer or major neurological disorders (Merikangas et al, 2011). Moreover, less than half of those with BD are adequately recognized and receive psychoactive treatments, particularly in the case of subjects living in lower income countries (Merikangas et al, 2011).

Social dysfunctions persist for long periods in many patients with BD even after the resolution of their manic or depressive episodes and also if affective symptoms are clinically absent (Basso et al, 2002; Thompson et al,

2005). Psychosocial impairment seems to be related with multiple factors including the disability to plan actions and behaviours, understand connection between life situations and emotions, use emotions as a resource for understanding interpersonal situations and accounting for important information and significant others.

Suicidal behaviour, frequently linked with MDD, is also associated with high psychological and social costs, and many billions of dollars are lost every year in terms of lost productivity, health and social care costs due to this complex phenomenon. Suicide is one of the most important cause of premature death, accounting for approximately one million of healthy life lost among teenagers and young adults every year. In overall, suicide deaths account for more than half of all violent deaths in the world -more than all deaths from wars and homicides combined (Pompili et al, 2012).

Although the recovery of personal and social functioning is generally accepted as an important clinical goal (Burns et al, 2007; Harvey et al, 2009), many criticisms may be mentioned when examining the current social impact of MDD worldwide and the failure of many treatments. These conditions still represent important public health concerns and many individuals, although experiencing only subthreshold affective symptoms that do not meet criteria required for the DSM-IV-TR (American Psychiatric Association, 2000) diagnosis, also report a significant psychosocial impairment and reduced quality of life. Moreover, treatment may be complicated in the presence of comorbidity with other psychiatric and medical conditions and needs to be individualized in most cases.

The present chapter aimed to examine the current literature about the impact of psychosocial impairment in patients with MDD trying to understand the real consequences of these disabling conditions on functional outcome and quality of life.

METHODS

A reference search was performed across the Medline and ScienceDirect databases (January 1980 and December 2012). The search used the following terms: "Affective disorders" OR "Mood disorders" AND "Major Depression" OR "Major Depressive Disorders" AND "Bipolar Disorders" AND "social impact" OR "psychosocial impairment". In addition, the reference lists of all papers identified were reviewed. Approximately 100 papers have been included in the present chapter. Included papers were all published in peer reviewed journals.

Where a title or abstract seemed to describe a study eligible for inclusion, the full article was obtained and examined to assess its relevance. Two independent researchers conducted a two-step literature search. Any discrepancies between the two reviewers who, blind to each other, examined the studies for the possible inclusion were resolved by consultations with a senior author.

RESULTS

The Psychosocial Impairment of Major Affective Disorders

Psychiatric disorders such as MDD and schizophrenia are often characterized by severe psychosocial impairment and reduced quality of life. During the last decades, psychosocial dysfunctions have been mainly described as related to schizophrenia and other psychotic disorders. However, impaired psychosocial functioning is also common in subjects with MDD.

Individual psychosocial functioning may be influenced by various factors. Previous studies investigating factors involved in psychosocial functioning in subjects with mental disorders highlighted the importance of neurocognitive deficits (Addington and Addington,1999; Green, 1996; Green et al, 2000), poor social skills and competencies (Möller et al., 2011) or stigmatization and other social barriers (Lysaker et al, 2007).

The link between impairments in social competence, social dysfunctions, psychopathology and neurocognitive dysfunctions has been clearly reported in schizophrenic patients (Bowie et al, 2008; Harvey et al, 2007; Dickinson et al, 2007) but has not been deeply investigated in MDD.

Recently, Iosifescu (2012) suggested that the association between cognitive deficits and functional impairment exists independently of mood symptoms although affective symptoms may be frequently associated with cognitive dysfunctions in the clinical practice.

Bottlender et al. (2012) investigated the association between psychopathological symptoms and impaired psychosocial functioning in affective, schizoaffective and schizophrenic disorders. Their findings indicated that higher levels of psychopathology were associated with higher functional impairment in almost all domains of psychosocial functioning across the three diagnostic groups. However, although the severity of problems in functioning appeared different among the three diagnostic subgroups, a similar pattern of impairment in psychosocial functioning has been reported.

The same level of impairment in terms of psychosocial functioning seems to suggest that disability is associated with the severity rather than the nature and quality of illness. Similar findings were reported by Rymaszewska et al. (2007) who found that the severity of psychopathological symptoms was the most significant factor in determining the level of social functioning independently of diagnosed mental disorders.

Catty et al. (2008) investigated vocational rehabilitation in patients with schizophrenic, schizoaffective and BD and found that remission of symptoms as assessed by the Positive and Negative Syndrome Scale (PANSS) was a significant predictor of working longer hours. As in other studies, psychiatric diagnoses did not relevantly predict vocational functioning (Catty et al, 2008).

However, whether among all affective disorders, there are some clinical conditions associated with a more pronounced psychosocial impairment compared to others is still quite unclear. Here, our aim was to analyze the level of social impairment associated with MDD and BD trying to identify, according to the current literature, whether these conditions are associated with different levels of disability and social disadvantages.

The Social Impact of MDD

Patients with MDD reported relevant psychosocial impairment that strongly affects their health-related quality of life (Ardal et al, 2012). Evidence suggested that subjects with MDD experience severe lifetime disability and poor quality of life (Papakostas et al, 2004). It's also well known that cognitive impairment may have negative implications on functional outcome and psychosocial impairment in patients with MDD.

Cognitive dysfunctions, no doubt, play a predominant role in enhancing psychosocial impairment in patients with MDD. Differences in terms of cognitive dysfunctions may affect not only psychosocial functioning but also treatment adherence as well as the possibility to benefit of rehabilitative activities. It may be very useful for clinicians to identify specific neurocognitive predictors of impaired psychosocial functioning and poor functional outcome in MDD patients. To date, only some studies have specifically investigated neuropsychological profile of subjects with MDD.

Acute episodes of MDD may be characterized by cognitive impairment involving dysfunctions in multiple cognitive domains, such as attention, memory and executive functions (Austin et al, 2001; Hammar and Ardal, 2009). Alterations in a variety of attention-related tasks have been frequently reported in the acute phases of illness but some studies suggested that patients with MDD reported impairments in attention-related tasks but not in automatic processing (Hammar and Ardal, 2009). Similarly, memory deficits involving both verbal and visual memory, verbal delayed memory, visuo-spatial memory, verbal working and long-term memory, working memory, and executive functioning have been commonly described in acute depression (Hammar and Ardal, 2009).

Moreover, other deficits have been demonstrated using psychometric instruments measuring inhibition, problem solving and planning, mental flexibility, verbal fluency, decision making, or the ability to inhibit one stimulus to facilitate processing of another source of information in these populations of patients (Hugdahl et al, 2009). Austin et al. (2001) reviewed the literature and suggested that the inability to shift mental set was the most important impairment affecting executive functioning in patients with MDD.

Initially, cognitive deficits were understood only in the context of acute mood episodes later recovering according to the general improvement of depressive symptoms. However, in the last decade longitudinal studies suggested that many subjects with MDD experienced persistent cognitive deficits even after significant improvement of acute depressive symptoms (Fava et al, 2006) and during the remitted phases of MDD (Hasselbalch et al, 2011). There are multiple cognitive domains of persistent impairment in remitted MDD subjects including alterations in sustained and selective attention, verbal memory, verbal fluency and executive function. Deficits are also reported as evaluated by tests providing a general estimation of global cognitive functioning (Hasselbalch et al, 2011).

Moreover, the extent of cognitive impairment during periods of remission in patients with MDD seems to be related to the number of previous depressive episodes (Kessing, 1998) and these impairments usually worsen with further MDD episodes (Brown et al, 1999; Sweeney et al, 2000). Also, the presence of persistent cognitive dysfunctions does not appear to be related to the use of antidepressant medications which were used (Gualtieri et al, 2006).

In a recent review, only 2 of 11 studies did not report persistent deficits in remitted MDD subjects (Hasselbalch et al, 2011). Even when cognitive deficits improve in remitted patients, their performance and social functioning remain below the level of healthy controls (Biringer et al, 2005). Acute episodes of MDD are associated with significant functional disability that generally persists even after improvement of depressive symptoms (Papakostas et al, 2004). Acute MDD episodes are associated with deficits in work performance, productivity, and absence of days due to sickness (Wang et al, 2004; Adler et al, 2006).

Such functional deficits have been traditionally understood as a consequence of mood symptoms and are thought to restore after depressive remission. Conversely, dysfunctions in family and social relations, leading to household strain, social irritability, financial strain, limitations in occupational functioning and poor health status (Papakostas et al, 2004) are thought to persist even after long periods of wellbeing.

Recent evidence suggested that improvement in functional status does not fully track improvement in depressive symptoms (Adler et al, 2006; Kennedy et al, 2007). Importantly, persistent cognitive impairment appears to play an important role in persistently impaired functional outcome in depression. Jaeger et al. (2006) reported that dysfunctions in attention, ideational fluency, non-verbal (visuo-spatial) and learning domains were strongly associated with life functional disability measured 6 months later.

In a recent study by Plaisier et al. (2010), the authors confirmed the association between psychopathology and work functioning among working individuals. Subjects having current depressive symptoms have been associated with a seven-fold higher risk of long-term absence and five-fold higher risk of impaired work performance when compared with those having current anxiety symptoms (that increased only a two-fold odds for long-term absence and impaired work performance).

Individuals with remitted depressive disorders reported both more absenteeism and decreased work performance than those with remitted anxiety disorders (who had decreased work performance but not more absenteeism). An higher severity of depressive symptoms was associated with an increased long-term absenteeism and impaired work performance.

In addition, the presence of comorbidities with anxiety disorders has been found as an important condition associated with elevated risks of poor work functioning. However, no studies have examined the independent effects of specific psychopathological variables (such as the effects of anxiety and depression) in a sample of psychiatric patients compared to healthy controls.

The economic impact of both anxiety and depressive disorders has been demonstrated to be enormous (Druss et al, 2000; Stewart et al, 2003). In subjects with depressive or anxiety disorders having an age between 18 and 65 years, 80% of the economic costs are due to the loss of working productivity (Smith et al, 2006).

In a recent study among employees of a large US information technology firm, depressive disorders accounted for 20%, and comorbid depression, anxiety and sleep problems even for 40% of the annual lost productivity costs (Kessler et al, 2008). Previous studies have found psychosocial (Coryell et al, 1993; Wells et al, 1989) and cognitive (Nakano et al, 2008; Paelecke-Habermann et al, 2005) deficits in subjects after acute depressive episodes indicating remaining subthreshold depressive symptoms which may affect work functioning.

Ormel et al. (2004) reported remaining effects in psychosocial disability among severe recurrent depressive disorders and suggested that individuals continued to recover from depressive disorders for many years (Mueller et al, 1996), further confirming that many patients with remitted depressive disorders may still have underlying subthreshold symptoms that may impact work functioning.

However, not all studies replicated these findings. Biringer et al. (2005) recently showed that improvement of acute depressive symptoms was positively correlated with improvement of long-term executive functioning.

Furthermore, most studies have shown that negative life events and social support were important factors in the functional outcome of MDD. There are at least two possible models able to explain the influence of social support on the development and course of major depression. First, the main effect model postulates that high levels of social support enhance a general positive environment which directly contribute to lower levels of depressive symptoms irrespective of current levels of stressors (Dumont and Provost, 1999). According to this model, several studies indicated that social support may exert a main effect on levels of depressive symptoms in adolescents (Bal et al, 2003; Burton et al, 2004; DuBois et al, 1994; Helsen et al, 2000; Holahan et al, 1995; Jackson and Warren, 2000; Slavin and Rainer, 1990; Windle, 1992; Zimmerman et al, 2000), although the type of social support which has been examined varied across studies. Second, indirect effect model (or buffering model) reports that high levels of social support buffer against the deleterious impact of stress on depressive symptoms (Cobb, 1976).

Relevantly, in the context of the buffering model, the beneficial impact of social support should be observed under conditions of high stress (Cohen, 2004). Aro et al. (1989) suggested that adolescents who exhibit low levels of parental or peer support are at greater risk to experience increases in psychosomatic symptoms following the occurrence of stressful life events than others. Results of further studies equally supported the buffering model

(DuBois et al, 1992, 1994; Henrich and Shahar, 2008; Jackson and Warren, 2000; Ystgaard et al, 1999).

Finally, many patients with MDD experience cognitive impairment not only in the acute phases of illness but also in remission as a result of subthreshold depressive symptoms or independently of mood symptoms; the presence of cognitive dysfunctions is frequently associated with increased psychosocial impairment and poor quality of life in these subjects.

The Social Impact of BD

BD is, among all psychiatric disorders, one of the most disabling condition worldwide (Murray and Lopez, 1996). Those with BD report lower rates of employment compared to healthy adults but the impact of this disabling illness is also critical on social functioning (Sanchez-Moreno et al, 2009; Simon et al, 2007; Elgie et al, 2007). Individuals with BD have fewer social interactions and smaller social networks than healthy subjects (Bauwens et al, 1991, 1998) and are less likely to achieve marriage or equivalent relationships compared to the general population (Judd and Akiskal, 2003).

These social impairments seem to persist also after acute episodes (Gitlin et al, 1995) and the presence of social dysfunctions indeed predicts shorter time to relapse (Bauwens et al, 1998). Reliable predictors of social disability in BD are still quite unclear although there is converging evidence suggesting that bipolar depression, even at a subsyndromal level, may predict global disability in BD (Gitlin et al, 1995; Judd et al, 2005). Further predictors of global disability including social dysfunctions, the presence of psychotic features, comorbid substance abuse, and neurocognitive impairment (Wingo et al, 2009; Depp et al, 2008; 2009) have also been described.

Nevertheless, progress in specifying the direct and interactive contributors to social disability in BD has been limited by the measurement of social functioning as well as by the small sample sizes that do not allow the use of multivariate approaches (Pope et al, 2007).

In a recent study, Depp et al. (2010) found that most of a large sample of outpatients with BD showed at least some social impairments on an observer-rated measure. Furthermore, nearly one-third of subjects exhibited impairments in social competence based on a performance-based measure of functioning. In multivariate analyses, the severity of depressive symptoms was the strongest correlate of observer-rated social functioning highlighting the need for effective treatments aimed to reduce bipolar depression. The authors suggested that, in overall, even among outpatients experiencing low severity of symptoms, social disability is quite common in BD and social disability should represent an important target for interventions.

Moreover, the subset of patients who shows impairment in social competence may benefit from interventions aimed to enhance social skills. Such impairments have been clearly associated to the presence of cognitive dysfunctions which have been well demonstrated during acute or subsyndromal mood episodes: deficits of verbal and visual memory as well as executive functions have been commonly described during acute depressive episodes (Malhi et al, 2007) whereas attention and executive dysfunctions have been frequently reported during mania (Martinez-Aran et al, 2004).

There is now converging evidence that patients with BD exhibit cognitive impairments even when they are in euthymic states (Malhi et al, 2007). Approximately 40–60% of bipolar patients are cognitively impaired at a level deemed to be clinically relevant, even during periods of affective remission (Martino et al, 2008). Savitz et al. (2005) reviewed 40 studies examining neurocognitive functions in euthymic subjects with BD. Only 3 of these 40 studies failed to detect cognitive impairment in euthymic bipolar patients suggesting that cognitive impairment may represent a permanent trait in this population and not a feature related only to acute mood episodes.

Cognitive dysfunctions are present in both BD type I and II during euthymia but may be more severe among bipolar I patients (Simonsen et al, 2008). Most of bipolar patients showed difficulties with attention, memory and executive functions. Meta-analytic studies have reported medium-to-large effect sizes of cognitive deficits in euthymic bipolar patients compared to healthy individuals (Robinson et al, 2006; Bora et al, 2009). Similarly, medium-to-large impairments were found in attention and processing speed, episodic memory, and executive functioning in a meta-analysis of 28 studies assessing cognitive functioning in 1026 euthymic bipolar patients and 1384 healthy controls matched for age, sex, education and estimated IQ (Mann-Wrobel et al, 2011). Recent meta-analytic studies consistently showed moderate-to-large deficits in sustained attention, psychomotor speed, verbal learning and memory, abstraction and executive functioning as core dysfunctions in remitted bipolar patients (Robinson et al, 2006; Bora et al, 2009; Mann-Wrobel et al, 2011).

Longitudinal findings suggested that cognitive deficits, present at the first episode, usually worsened over time with repeated bipolar mood episodes (Robinson and Ferrier, 2006). Indeed, a large number of reports correlated neuropsychological deficits with both the number of affective episodes and overall duration of bipolar illness (Denicoff et al, 1999; Mann-Wrobel et al, 2011). Therefore it's likely that cognitive dysfunctions in BD are related to functional (and possibly structural) neurodegenerative changes in specific brain areas. This is consistent with some neuroimaging studies demonstrating that the number of previous depressive and manic episodes has been associated with decreased size of cerebellar vermis (DelBello et al, 1999) and increased ventricular size (Strakowski et al, 2002).

However, considering that some cognitive deficits may be present at the first episode and even in first-degree relatives of patients with BD (Clark et al, 2005), it is possible that cognitive deficits may be related to aberrant neurodevelopment or a genetic vulnerability to develop bipolar illness. As mentioned, patients with BD also experience significant functional impairment, not only during acute manic, depressive or mixed episodes, but also during periods of remission (Fagiolini et al, 2005). MacQueen et al. (2001) reported that 30–60% of individuals with BD failed to regain full functioning in occupational and social domains after remission of mood episodes. Of 134 bipolar patients, only 24% achieved functional recovery within a year of hospitalization for a manic or mixed episode (Keck et al, 1998).

Multiple studies suggested that functional impairment in euthymic patients with BD may be related to persistent neuropsychological deficits. Indeed, the severity of cognitive deficits in asymptomatic patients with BD has been significantly associated with poor psychosocial functioning, such as inability to hold a job (Atre-Vaidya et al, 1998). However, residual depressive symptoms are also crucial in determining the severity of functional disability. Bowie et al. (2010) found that, in a sample of 130 bipolar patients, severity of depression and cognitive impairment was similar. Moreover, depression was negatively associated with work skills and interpersonal functioning (as measured by the Specific level of Functioning Scale) (Bowie et al, 2010).

In a recent study including 283 patients with BD, Iosifescu et al. (2011) suggested that cognitive deficits and depression scores were independently associated with quality of life and functional outcome measures even after controlling for significant variables such as age, gender, and severity of mania. Martinez-Aràn et al. (2004) in a cross-sectional study compared 4 groups: manic or hypomanic bipolars, depressed bipolars, euthymic bipolars, and healthy controls using a neuropsychological test battery. Each of the three bipolar groups showed significant impairments in verbal memory and executive functions compared to controls. The most recent meta-analytic study on this topic considered 45 studies comparing 1423 euthymic bipolar patients with 1524 healthy controls (Bora et al, 2009). The authors showed group differences with medium to large effect sizes for measures related to executive functions, verbal memory, psychomotor speed, and sustained attention.

In overall, cognitive deficits may play an important role on social functioning and the course of illness. Most of studies seems to sustain the hypothesis that cognitive impairments exist also in euthymia although they are substantially different from those of manic or depressive state (Latalova et al, 2011). Importantly, these deficits have a significant impact on occupational ability and social integration.

Wingo et al. (2009) in a recent review identified 13 studies addressing the relationship between cognitive impairments and functional outcome in euthymic bipolar patients compared with healthy controls. Significant relationships between cognitive impairments and functional outcome have been reported in 12 of the 13 studies reviewed.

Strategies to Reduce the Impact of Psychosocial Impairment in MDD: Implications for Prevention

Improving control of affective symptoms may represent an important strategy to ameliorate functional outcome of subjects with MDD (Iosifescu, 2012). Therefore, aggressive treatment of affective symptoms is highly recommended as an important tool for optimizing psychosocial functioning and functional outcome in MDD and other psychiatric conditions. However, other alternative strategies may be considered.

First, social networks and social support should be enhanced as they were found to be beneficial in reducing the impact of stress on precipitation of mental disorders (Cobb, 1976; Cohen and Wills, 1985; Thoits, 1986). An adequate social network may be defined as an objective assessment of the size and frequency of interactions with one's friends or relatives whereas social support is generally known as a subjective perceived quality of the support as individually appraised (Vaux, 1988). However, it is not clear whether social networks and social support may exert a direct effect (e.g. the effect of social networks and support on psychiatric disorders irrespective of the presence/absence of a significant life event), or a stress-buffering effect (i.e. the interaction between stressful life events and social networks/social support, or how social networks and social support vary among those with or without life events and how this affects mental disorders) or both of these effects on mental illness.

In 1985 Cohen suggested that measures of social support had a stress-buffering effect whereas measures of social networks had a direct effect on mental illness. However, Paykel (1994) suggested that social support had both direct and stress-buffering effects on depression (he believed that low support enhanced the risk to develop depression whereas high support could buffer the effect of stress).

Other researchers (Dalgard et al, 2006) suggested that low social support was associated with an increased risk for depression and, recently, Maulik et al. (2010) found that social support from friends or relatives was significantly associated with reduced odds of panic disorder and psychological distress after negative life events. They confirmed that social networks or social support had no significant stress-buffering effect and almost no direct or buffering effect on MDD, generalized anxiety disorder and alcohol abuse/dependence disorder.

Also, another relevant strategy aimed to reduce the impact of psychosocial impairment in MDD is to consider cognitive residual deficits after acute mood episodes as crucial target for treatment interventions aimed to improve functional outcome.

The nature and clinical course of cognitive dysfunctions in the various subtypes of MDD are presumably different. The possibility to track differential trajectories of illness associated with a more favorable/unfavorable outcome may be of particular interest for clinicians. Also, the relationships between mood symptoms, cognitive impairment and functional deficits (Iosifescu, 2012) must not be ignored. Clinicians have to investigate more carefully the interactions between neuropsychological profile (using both neuropsychological tests and self-report instruments) as well as psychopathology in patients with MDD.

Treatment strategies focused on cognitive dysfunctions should be used in clinical practice for optimizing functional outcomes. Recently, Murrough et al. (2011) reviewed the literature suggesting that several pharmacological and non-pharmacological interventions have clearly demonstrated to improve cognitive dysfunctions in depression and also they showed beneficial effects in improving functional outcomes.

The present chapter should be considered in the light of the following limitations. First, many of the reported studies include relatively small and heterogeneous samples, the results of which should be not generalized. In addition, studies examining potential contributors to social disability in BD have been limited by the measurement of social functioning as well as small sample sizes that did not allow the use of multivariate approaches (Pope et al, 2007). Important indicators of social functioning, such as marital status or social network size, are influenced by several factors such as stigma or environmental opportunities that are difficult to divide by the effects related to illness.

Moreover, subjective measures of social functioning (e.g. social support) are influenced by mood state at the time of assessment and this may affect estimates of the impact of affective disorders on social functioning. Also, previous research have not separately analyzed the impact of social competence and other factors such as cognitive and emotional skills needed for social interactions on social disability. Moreover, not all studies used the same criteria to evaluate the nature and severity of psychosocial impairment in MDD.

Finally, most of patients were taking psychoactive medications when they were recruited in the studies and this could have biased both their cognitive performance and psychosocial functioning.

CONCLUSION

Various psychiatric conditions are characterized by relevant psychosocial impairment and have a significant impact on quality of life. Among these, MDD, no doubt, represent relevant public health concerns. The severity of functional deficits and psychosocial impairment in patients with MDD is directly associated with the presence of both affective symptoms (especially depressive symptoms) and cognitive dysfunctions. Cognitive dysfunctions seem to be influenced by the presence of affective symptoms but they may be also present independently of affective symptoms in patients with MDD. Therefore, MDD appear to have both a direct and indirect impact on psychosocial functioning (the latter mediated by the effect of mood symptoms on cognition). In overall, the link between affective symptoms, cognitive impairment and functional deficits appears to be consistent in most patients with MDD.

The presence of cognitive deficits and residual symptoms (both residual depression and mania) represent an important target for treatment interventions aimed to improve functional outcomes. Both pharmacological and non-pharmacological strategies focused on cognitive deficits should be used to ameliorate quality of life and reduce the burden of psychosocial impairment in patients with MDD.

As suggested by Bottlender et al. (2012), a multidimensional assessment of psychosocial dysfunctions using comprehensive instruments is highly recommended in the clinical practice as it may provide a deep understanding into the complexity of impaired social functioning in patients with MDD.

However, further research are needed to investigate the role of cognitive impairment in affective disorders as well as its relation with emotional dysregulation and biological/environmental risk factors. Research aimed to investigate cognitive impairments in MDD may yield important revisions of our current clinical approach to the these disabling conditions.

REFERENCES

Addington J, Addington D. Neurocognitive and social functioning in schizophrenia. *Schizophr. Bull.,* 1999; 25(1):173–182.

Adler DA, McLaughlin TJ, Rogers WH, Chang H, Lapitsky L, Lerner D. Job performance deficits due to depression. *Am. J. Psychiatry* 2006; 163: 1569–1576.

American Psychiatric Association. *Diagnostic and Statistical Manual of Mental Disorders, Text Revision (4th ed).* Washingon DC: American Psychiatric Association, 2000.

Ardal G, Lund A, Hammar A. Health-related quality of life in recurrent major depressive disorder-A 10-year follow-up study. *Nord. J. Psychiatry* 2012 (in press).

Aro H, Hanninen V, Paronen O. Social support, life events and psychosomatic symptoms among 14–16-years-old adolescents. *Soc. Sci. Med.,* 1989; 29: 1051–1056.

Atre-Vaidya N, Taylor MA, Seidenberg M, Reed R, Perrine A, Glick-Oberwise F. Cognitive deficits, psychopathology, and psychosocial functioning in bipolar mood disorder. *Neuropsychiatry Neuropsychol. Behav. Neurol.,* 1998;11 (3):120–126.

Austin MP, Mitchell P, Goodwin GM. Cognitive deficits in depression: possible implications for functional neuropathology. *Br. J. Psychiatry,* 2001;178:200–206.

Bal S, Crombez G, Oost PV, Debourdeaudhuij I. The role of social support in well-being and coping with self-reported stressful events in adolescents. *Child Abuse Negl.,* 2003; 27: 1377–1395.

Basso MR, Lowery N, Neel J. Neuropsychological impairment among manic, depressed, and mixed-episode inpatients with bipolar disorder. *Neuropsychology,* 2002; 16: 84-91.

Bauwens F, Tracy A, Pardoen D, Vander Elst M, Mendlewicz J. Social adjustment of remitted bipolar and unipolar out-patients. A comparison with age- and sexmatched controls. *Br. J. Psychiatry,* 1991; 159: 239–244.

Bauwens F, Pardoen D, Staner L, Dramaix M, Mendlewicz J. Social adjustment and the course of affective illness: a one-year controlled longitudinal study involving bipolar and unipolar outpatients. *Depress. Anxiety,* 1998; 8: 50–57.

Biringer E, Lundervold A, Stordal K, Mykletun A, Egeland J, Bottlender R, et al. Executive function improvement upon remission of recurrent unipolar depression. *Eur. Arch. Psychiatry Clin. Neurosci.,* 2005; 255: 373–380.

Bora E, Yucel M, Pantelis C. Cognitive endophenotypes of bipolar disorder: a meta-analysis of neuropsychological deficits in euthymic patients and their first-degree relatives. *J. Affect. Disord.,* 2009; 113: 1–20.

Bottlender R, Strauss A and Möller H-J. Association between psychopathology and problems of psychosocial functioning in the long-term outcome of patients diagnosed with schizophrenic, schizoaffective and affective disorders. *Eur. Arch. Psychiatry Clin. Neurosci.,* 2012 (in press).

Bowie CR, Depp C, McGrath JA, Wolyniec P, Mausbach BT, Thornquist MH, et al. Prediction of real-world functional disability in chronic mental disorders: a comparison of schizophrenia and bipolar disorder. *Am. J. Psychiatry,* 2010; 167(9): 1116–1124.

Bowie CR, Leung WW, Reichenberg A, et al. Predicting schizophrenia patients' real-world behavior with specific neuropsychological and functional capacity measures. *Biol. Psychiatry,* 2008; 63: 505-511.

Brown ES, Rush AJ, McEwen BS. Hippocampal remodeling and damage by corticosteroids: implications for mood disorders. *Neuropsychopharmacology,* 1999; 21: 474–484.

Buist-Bouwman MA, de GR, Vollebergh WA, Ormel J. Comorbidity of physical and mental disorders and the effect on work-loss days. *Acta Psychiatr. Scand.,* 2005; 111: 436–443.

Burdick KE, Goldberg JF, Harrow M. Neurocognitive dysfunction and psychosocial outcome in patients with bipolar I disorder at 15-year follow-up. *Acta Psychiatr. Scand.,* 2010;122(6):499–506.

Burns T, Patrick D. Social functioning as an outcome measure in schizophrenia studies. *Acta Psychiatr. Scand.,* 2007;116(6):403–418.

Burton E, Stice E, Seely JR. A prospective test of the stress-buffering model of depression in adolescent girls: no support once again. *J. Consul. Clin. Psychol.,* 2004; 72: 689–697.

Catty J, Lissouba P, White S, Becker T, Drake RE, Fioritti A, et al. Predictors of employment for people with severe mental illness. *Br. J. Psychiatry* 2008;192:224–231.

Clark L, Sarna A, Goodwin GM. Impairment of executive function but not memory in first-degree relatives of patients with bipolar I disorder and in euthymic patients with unipolar depression. *Am. J. Psychiatry,* 2005; 162 (10): 1980–1982.

Cobb S. Social support as a moderator of life stress. *Psychosom. Med.,* 1976; 38: 300–314.

Cohen S, Wills TA. Stress, social support, and the buffering hypothesis. *Psychol. Bull.,* 1985;98:310–357.

Cohen S. Social relationships and health. *Am. Psychol.,* 2004; 676–684.

Coryell W, Scheftner W, Keller M, Endicott J, Maser J, Klerman GL. The enduring psychosocial consequences of mania and depression. *Am. J. Psychiatry,* 1993; 150: 720–727.

Dalgard OS, Dowrick C, Lehtinen V Vazquez-Barquero JL, Casey P, Wilkinson G, et al. Negative life events, social support and gender difference in depression: multinational community survey with data from the ODIN study. *Soc. Psychiatry Psychiatr. Epidemiol.,* 2006;41:444–451.

DelBello MP, Strakowski SM, Zimmerman ME, Hawkins JM, Sax KW. MRI analysis of the cerebellum in bipolar disorder: a pilot study. *Neuropsychopharmacology,* 1999; 21 (1): 63–68.

Denicoff KD, Ali SO, Mirsky AF, Smith-Jackson EE, Leverich GS, Duncan CC, et al. Relationship between prior course of illness and neuropsychological functioning in patients with bipolar disorder. *J. Affect. Disord.,* 1999; 56: 67–73.

Depp CA, Cain AE, Palmer BW, Moore DJ, Eyler LT, Lebowitz BD, et al. Assessment of medication management ability in middle-aged and older adults with bipolar disorder. *J. Clin. Psychopharmacol.,*2008;28:225–229.

Depp CA, Mausbach BT, Eyler LT, Palmer BW, Cain AE, Lebowitz BD, et al. Performance based and subjective measures of functioning in middle aged and older adults with bipolar disorder. *J. Nerv. Ment. Dis.,* 2009; 197: 471–475.

Depp CA, Mausbach BT, Harvey PD, Bowie CR, Wolyniec PS, Thornquist MH, et al. Social competence and observer-rated social functioning in bipolar disorder. *Bipolar Disord.,* 2010:12: 843–850.

Dickinson D, Bellack AS, Gold JM. Social/communication skills, cognition, and vocational functioning in schizophrenia. *Schizophr. Bull.,* 2007; 33: 1213–1220.

Druss BG, Rosenheck RA, Sledge WH. Health and disability costs of depressive illness in a major U.S. corporation. *Am. J. Psychiatry* 2000;157: 1274–1278.

DuBois DL, Felner R, Brand S, Adan A, Evans E. A prospective study of life stress, social support, and adaptation in early adolescence. *Child Dev.,* 1992; 63: 542–557.

DuBois DL, Felner RD, Meares H, Krier M. Prospective investigation of the effects of socioeconomic disadvantage, life stress, and social support on early adolescent adjustment. *J. Abnorm. Psychol.,* 1994; 103: 511–522.

Dumont M, Provost MA. Resilience in adolescents: protective role of social support, coping strategies, self-esteem, and social activities on experience of stress and depression. *J. Youth Adolesc.,* 1999; 28:343–363.

Dumont M, Provost MA. Resilience in adolescents: protective role of social support, coping strategies, self-esteem, and social activities on experience of stress and depression. *J. Youth Adolesc.,* 1999; 28; 343–363.

Elgie R, Morselli PL. Social functioning in bipolar patients: the perception and perspective of patients, relatives and advocacy organizations – a review. *Bipolar Disord.,* 2007; 9: 144–157.

Fagiolini A, Kupfer DJ, Masalehdan A, Scott JA, Houck PR, Frank E. Functional impairment in the remission phase of bipolar disorder. *Bipolar Disord.,* 2005; 7 (3): 281–285.

Fava M, Graves LM, Benazzi F, Scalia MJ, Iosifescu DV, Alpert JE, et al. A cross-sectional study of the prevalence of cognitive and physical symptoms during long- term antidepressant treatment. *J. Clin. Psychiatry,* 2006; 67 (11): 1754–1759.

Gitlin M, Swendsen J, Heller T, Hammen C. Relapse and impairment in bipolar disorder. *Am. J. Psychiatry,* 1995; 152: 1635–1640.

Glozier N. Mental ill health and fitness for work. *Occup. Environ. Med.,* 2002; 59: 714–720.

Goetzel RZ, Long SR, Ozminkowski RJ, Hawkins K, Wang S, Lynch W. Health, absence, disability, and presenteeism cost estimates of certain physical and mental health conditions affecting U.S. employers. *J. Occup. Environ. Med.,* 2004; 46: 398–412.

Green MF. What are the functional consequences of neurocognitive deficits in schizophrenia? *Am. J. Psychiatry* 1996;153(3):321–330.

Green MF, Kern RS, Braff DL, Mintz J. Neurocognitive deficits and functional outcome in schizophrenia: are we measuring the ''right stuff''? *Schizophr. Bull.,* 2000; 26(1):119–136.

Gualtieri TC, Johnson LG, Benedict KB. Neurocognition in depression: Patients on and off medication versus healthy comparison subjects. *J. Neuropsychiatry Clin. Neurosci.,* 2006; 18: 217–225.

Hammar A, Ardal G. Cognitive functioning in major depression—a summery. *Front. Hum. Neurosci.,* 2009; 3(26): 1–7.

Harvey PO, Le Bastard G, Pochon JB, Levy R, Allilaire JF, Dubois B, et al. Executive functions and updating of the contents of working memory in unipolar depressions. *J. Psychiatr. Res.,* 2004; 38: 567–576.

Harvey PD, Velligan DI, Bellack AS. Performance-based measures of functional skills: usefulness in clinical treatment studies. *Schizophr. Bull.,* 2007; 33: 1138–1148.

Harvey PD, Bellack AS. Toward a terminology for functional recovery in schizophrenia. *Schizophr. Bull.,* 2009;35(2):300–306.

Hasselbalch BJ, Knorr U, Kessing LV. Cognitive impair- ment in the remitted state of unipolar depressive disorder: a systematic review. *J. Affect. Disord.,* 2011; 134 (1–3): 20–31.

Helsen M, Vollebergh W, Meeus W. Social support from parents and friends and emotional problems in adolescence. *J. Youth Adolesc.,* 2000; 29; 319–335.

Henrich CC, Shahar G. Social support buffers the effects of terrorism on adolescent depression: findings from Sderot, Israel. *J. Am. Acad. Child Adolesc. Psychiatry,* 2008; 47: 1073–1076.

Holahan CJ, Valentiner DP, Moos RH. Parental support, coping strategies, and psychological adjustment: an integrative model with late adolescents. *J. Youth Adolesc.,* 1995; 24: 633–648.

Hugdahl K, Westerhausen R, Alho K, Medvedev S, Laine M, Hämäläinen H. Attention and cognitive control: unfold- ing the dichotic listening story. *Scand. J. Psychol.,* 2009; 50: 11–22.

Iosifescu DV, Leon AC, Sylvia LG, Bowden CL, Ostacher MJ, Calabrese JR, et al. Cognitive deficits are an important determinant of functional deficits in bipolar disorder: baseline results from LiTMUS. *Bipolar Disord.,* 2011; 13 (s1): 22.

Iosifescu DV. The relation between mood, cognition and psychosocial functioningin psychiatric disorders. *Eur. Neuropsychopharmacol.,* 2012; 22: S499–S504.

Jackson Y, Warren JS. Appraisal, social support, and life events: predicting outcome behavior in School-Age Children. *Child Dev.,* 2000; 71: 1441–1457.

Jaeger J, Berns S, Uzelac S, Davis-Conway S. Neurocognitive deficits and disability in major depressive disorder. *Psychiatry Res.,* 2006; 145: 39–48.

Judd LL, Akiskal HS. The prevalence and disability of bipolar spectrum disorders in the US population: re-analysis of the ECA database taking into account subthreshold cases. *J. Affect. Disord.,* 2003; 73: 123–131.

Judd LL, Akiskal HS, Schettler PJ, Endicott J, Leon AC, Solomon DA, et al. Psychosocial disability in the course of bipolar I and II disorders: a prospective, comparative, longitudinal study. *Arch. Gen. Psychiatry,* 2005; 62: 1322–1330.

Judd LL, Schettler PJ, Solomon DA, Maser JD, Coryell W, Endicott J, et al. Psychosocial disability and work role function compared across the long-term course of bipolar I, bipolar II and unipolar major depressive disorders. *J. Affect. Disord.,* 2008;108(1– 2):49–58.

Keck PE Jr, McElroy SL, Strakowski SM, West SA, Sax KW, Hawkins JM, et al. 12-month outcome of patients with bipolar disorder following hospitalization for a manic or mixed episode. *Am. J. Psychiatry,* 1998; 155: 646–652.

Kennedy N, Foy F, Sherazi R, McDonough M, McKeon P. Long-term social functioning after depression treated by psy- chiatrists: a review. *Bipolar Disord.,* 2007; 9: 25–37.

Kessing LV. Cognitive impairment in the euthymic phase of affective disorder. *Psychol. Med.,* 1998; 28: 1027–1038.

Kessler RC, Frank RG. The impact of psychiatric disorders on work loss days. *Psychol. Med.,* 1997; 27: 861–873.

Kessler R, White LA, Birnbaum H, Qiu Y, Kidolezi Y, Mallett D, et al. Comparative and interactive effects of depression relative to other health problems on work performance in the workforce of a large employer. *J. Occup. Environ. Med.,* 2008; 50; 809–816.

Latalova K, Prasko J, Diveky T, Velartova H. Cognitive impairment in bipolar disorder. *Biomed. Pap. Med. Fac. Univ. Palacky. Olomouc. Czech. Repub.,* 2011;155(1):19-26.

Lim D, Sanderson K, Andrews G. Lost productivity among full-time workers with mental disorders. *J. Mental. Health Policy Econ.,* 2000; 3: 139–146.

Lysaker PH, Davis LW, Warman DM, Strasburger A, Beattie N. Stigma, social function and symptoms in schizophrenia and schizoaffective disorder: associations across 6 months. *Psychiatry Res.,* 2007; 149(1–3):89–95.

MacQueen GM, Young LT, Joffe RT. A review of psychosocial outcome in patients with bipolar disorder. *Acta Psychiatr. Scand.*, 2001; 103 (3): 163–170.

Malhi GS, Ivanovski B, Hadzi-Pavlovic D, Mitchell PB, Vieta E, Sachdev P. Neuropsychological deficits and functional impairment in bipolar depression, hypomania and euthymia. *Bipolar Disord.*, 2007; 9 (1–2): 114–125.

Mann-Wrobel MC, Carreno JT, Dickinson D. Meta-analysis of neuropsychological functioning in euthymic bipolar disorder: an update and investigation of moderator variables. *Bipolar Disord.*, 2011; 13 (4): 334–342.

Martinez-Aràn A, Vieta E, Reinares M, Colom F, Torrent C, Sánchez-Moreno J, et al. Cognitive function across manic or hypomanic, depressed, and euthymic states in bipolar disorder. *Am. J. Psychiatry*, 2004; 161:262–270.

Martino DJ, Strejilevich SA, Scápola M, Igoa A, Marengo E, Ais ED, et al. Heterogeneity in cognitive functioning among patients with bipolar disorder. *J. Affect. Disord.*, 2008; 109: 149–156.

Maulik PK, Eaton WW, Bradshaw CP. The effect of social networks and social support on common mental disorders following specific life events. *Acta Psychiatr. Scand.*, 2010: 122: 118–128.

Merikangas KR, Jin R, He JP, Kessler RC, Lee S, Sampson NA, et al. Prevalence and correlates of bipolar spectrum disorder in the world mental health survey initiative. *Arch. Gen. Psychiatr.*, 2011;68(3):241–251.

Möller HJ, Jäger M, Riedel M, Obermeier M, Strauss A, Bottlender R. The Munich 15-year follow-up study (MUFUSSAD) on first-hospitalized patients with schizophrenic or affective disorders: comparison of psychopathological and psychosocial course and outcome and prediction of chronicity. *Eur. Arch. Psychiatry Clin. Neurosci.*, 2011; 260(5):367–384.

Mueller TI, Keller MB, Leon AC, Solomon DA, Shea MT, Coryell W, et al. Recovery after 5 years of unremitting major depressive disorder. *Arch. Gen. Psychiatry*, 1996; 53: 794–799.

Mueser KT, Bellack AS, Morrison RL, Wixted JT. Social competence in schizophrenia: premorbid adjustment, social skill, and domains of functioning. *J. Psychiatr. Res.*, 1990; 24(1):51–63.

Murray C, Lopez A. *Global Burden of Disease.* Geneva: Harvard University Press, 1996.

Murray CJL, Lopez AD, editors. *The global burden of disease: a comprehensive assessment of mortality and disability from disease, injuries, and risk factors in 1990 and projected to 2020.*, Cambridge, MA: Harvard University Press, 1996.

Murrough JW, Iacoviello B, Neumeister A, Charney DS, Iosifescu DV. Cognitive dysfunction in depression *Neurobiol. Learn. Mem.,* 2011;96(4):553-563.

Nakano Y, Baba H, Maeshima H, Kitajima A, Sakai Y, Baba K, et al. Executive dysfunction in medicated, remitted state of major depression. *J. Affect. Disord.,* 2008; 111: 46–51.

O'Neill E, McNamee R, Agius R, Gittins M, Hussey L, Turner S. The validity and reliability of diagnoses of work-related mental ill-health. *Occup. Environ. Med.,* 2008; 65: 726–731.

Ormel J, Oldehinkel AJ, Nolen WA, Vollebergh W. Psychosocial disability before, during, and after a major depressive episode: a 3-wave population-based study of state, scar, and trait effects. *Arch. Gen. Psychiatry,* 2004; 61: 387–392.

Paelecke-Habermann Y, Pohl J, Leplow B. Attention and executive functions in remitted major depression patients. *J. Affect. Disord.,* 2005;89:125–135.

Papakostas GI, Petersen T, Mahal Y, Mischoulon D, Nierenberg AA, Fava M. Quality of life assessments in major depressive disorder: a review of the literature. *Gen. Hosp. Psychiatry,* 2004; 26: 13–17.

Paykel ES. Life events, social support and depression. *Acta Psychiatr. Scand. Suppl.,* 1994;377:50–58.

Plaisier I, Beekman ATF, de Graaf R, Smit JH, van Dyck R, Penninx BW. Work functioning in persons with depressive and anxiety disorders: The role of specific psychopathological characteristics. *J. Affect. Disord.,* 2010; 125: 198–206.

Pompili M, Editor. *Suicide: a global perspective.* Bentham Science Publishers, pp. 1-278, 2012.

Pope M, Dudley R, Scott J. Determinants of social functioning in bipolar disorder. *Bipolar Disord.,* 2007; 9: 38–44.

Robinson LJ, Ferrier IN. Evolution of cognitive impair- ment in bipolar disorder: a systematic review of cross-sectional evidence. *Bipolar Disord.,* 2006; 8;103–116.

Robinson LJ, Ferrier IN. Evolution of cognitive impairment in bipolar disorder: a systematic review of cross-sectional evidence. *Bipolar Disord.,* 2006; 8: 103–116.

Rymaszewska J, Jarosz-Nowak J, Kiejna A, Kallert T, Schützwohl M, Priebe S, et al. Social disability in different mental disorders. *Eur. Psychiatry* 2007; 22(3):160–166.

Sanchez-Moreno J, Martìnez-Aràn A, Tabares-Seisdedos R, Torrent C, Vieta E, Ayuso-Mateos JL. Functioning and disability in bipolar disorder: an extensive review. *Psychother. Psychosom.*, 2009; 78: 285–297.

Savitz J, Solms M, Ramesar R. Neuropsychological dysfunction in bipolar affective disorder: a critical opinion. *Bipolar Disord.*, 2005; 7(3):216–235.

Simon GE, Bauer MS, Ludman EJ, Operskalski BH, Unutzer J. Mood symptoms, functional impairment, and disability in people with bipolar disorder: specific effects of mania and depression. *J. Clin. Psychiatry,* 2007; 68: 1237– 1245.

Simonsen C, Sundet K, Vaskinn A, Birkenaes AB, Engh JA, Hansen CF, et al. Neurocognitive profiles in bipolar I and bipolar II disorder: differences in pattern and magnitude of dysfunction. *Bipolar Disord.,* 2008; 10: 245–255.

Slavin LA, Rainer KL. Gender differences in emotional support and depressive symptoms among adolescents: a prospective analysis. *Am. J. Community Psychol.,* 1990; 18: 407–421.

Smith F, Cuijpers P, Oostenbrink J, Batelaan N, de GR, Beekman A. Costs of nine common mental disorders: implications for curative and preventive psychiatry. *J. Ment. Health Policy Econ.,* 2006; 9: 193–200.

Stewart WF, Ricci JA, Chee E, Hahn SR, Morganstein D. Cost of lost productive work time among US workers with depression. *JAMA,* 2003; 289: 3135–3144.

Strakowski SM, DelBello MP, Zimmerman ME, Getz GE, Mills NP, Ret J, et al. Ventricular and periventricular structural volumes in first- versus multiple-episode bipolar disorder. *Am. J. Psychiatry,* 2002; 159 (11): 1841–1847.

Sweeney JA, Kmiec JA, Kupfer DJ. Neuropsychologic impairments in bipolar and unipolar mood disorders on the CANTAB neurocognitive battery. *Biol. Psychiatry,* 2000; 48:674–684.

Thoits PA. Social support as coping assistance. *J. Consult. Clin. Psychol.,* 1986;54:416–423.

Thompson JM, Gallagher P, Hughes JH. Neurocognitive impairment in euthymic patients with bipolar affective disorder. *Br. J. Psychiatry,* 2005; 186: 32-40.

Vaux A. *Social support: theory, research and intervention.* New York: Praeger, 1988.

Verow P, Hargreaves C. Healthy workplace indicators: costing reasons for sickness absence within the UK National Health Service. *Occup. Med. (Lond.),* 2000; 50: 251–257.

Waghorn G, Chant D, King R. Work-related self-efficacy among community residents with psychiatric disabilities. *Am. J. Psychiatr. Rehabil.,* 2005; 10: 275–300.

Wang J, Adair CE, Patten SB. Mental health and related disability among workers: a population-based study. *Am. J. Ind. Med.,* 2006; 49: 514–522.

Wang PS, Beck AL, Berglund P, McKenas DK, Pronk NP, Simon GE, et al. Effects of major depression on moment-in-time work performance. *Am. J. Psychiatry,* 2004; 161: 1885–1891.

Weinstock LM, Miller IW. Functional impairment as a predictor of short-term symptom course in bipolar I disorder. *Bipolar Disord.,* 2008; 10: 437–442.

Wells KB, Stewart A, Hays RD, Burnam MA, Rogers W, Daniels M, et al. The functioning and well-being of depressed patients. Results from the Medical Outcomes Study. *JAMA,* 1989; 262: 914–919.

Windle M. A longitudinal study of stress buffering for adolescent problem behaviors. *Dev. Psychol.,* 1992; 28: 522–530.

Wingo AP, Harvey PD, Baldessarini R. Neurocognitive impairment in bipolar disorder patients: functional implications. *Bipolar Disord.,* 2009; 11(2):113-125.

Ystgaard M, Tambs K, Dalgard OS. Life stress, social support and psychological distress in late adolescence: a longitudinal study. *Soc. Psychiatry Psychiatr. Epidemiol.,* 1999; 34: 12–19.

Zimmerman MA, Ramirez-Valles J, Zapert KM, Maton KI. A longitudinal study of stress-buffering effects for urban African-American male adolescent problem behaviors and mental health. *J. Community Psychol.,* 2000; 28: 17–33.

In: Affective Disorders
Editor: Linda D. Hambrick
ISBN: 978-1-62618-402-2

Chapter 4

THE GENDER DIFFERENCE IN DEPRESSIVE PREVALENCE RESULTS FROM HIGH PREVALENCE AMONG WOMEN OF DEPRESSION ASSOCIATED WITH SOMATIC SYMPTOMS DEVELOPING AT ADOLESCENCE IN RESPONSE TO PSYCHOSOCIAL ISSUES

Brett Silverstein
Department of Psychology
City College of New York, NY, US

ABSTRACT

Several lines of research suggest that the gender difference in depressive prevalence is due to the higher prevalence among women of a distinct depressive phenotype comprised of depression, disordered eating, body dissatisfaction, headaches, sleep problems, and fatigue that develops at adolescence. Furthermore, research shows that this phenotype is rooted in response to psychosocial issues particularly confronting contemporary women. First, women exhibit higher prevalence of all of these symptoms and, in all cases, the gender difference begins during adolescence as a result of dramatic increases in symptoms among females compared to males. Second, all of these somatic symptoms are more strongly related to depression among females than among males and this pattern too develops at adolescence. Third, all of these symptoms have been shown to have increased in prevalence over recent years among young women but not, or much less so, among men. Fourth, the variation among cohorts over the course of most of the twentieth century has been found to be similar between the gender difference in the prevalence of depression, the incidence of anorexia among young women, and the correlation between scores on depression inventories and the frequency of severe headache reported by women, three variables that would be expected to covary if a single disorder comprised of the symptoms discussed here afflicts women. These variations have been found to track historical changes in women's roles that probably led to an increase in the number of young women who were distressed by the limitations that had traditionally been placed on women. This suggests the possibility that the syndrome comprised of these symptoms might be rooted in psychosocial forces related to the dramatic changes in roles experienced by women in recent decades. Fifth, several studies have found that young women who report attitudes indicative of recognizing limitations placed upon them due to traditional gender roles, such as feeling that males have more opportunities than females or that their fathers exhibited preferences for males, exhibit high prevalence of depression accompanied by the additional symptoms listed above. Sixth, in self-report studies and large representative epidemiologic samples, this phenotype has been found to represent much of the higher prevalence of depression among women.

A large number of studies of depression as well as studies of such somatic symptoms as eating disorders, poor body image, headache, insomnia, and fatigue exhibit a similar pattern of results. First of all, women have been found to exhibit higher prevalence of all of these symptoms and, in all cases, the gender difference in prevalence has been found during adolescence as a result of dramatic increases in symptoms among females compared to males (e.g. depression, Ge, Conger and Elder, 2001; eating disorders, Ledoux, Choquet and Flament, 1989; body dissatisfaction, Mancilla-Diaz et al., 2009; headaches, Abu-Arefeh and Russell, 1994; insomnia, Johnson, Roth, Schultz and Breslau, 2006; fatigue, ter Wolbeek, van Doornen, Kavelaars and Heijnen, 2006). One possible explanation for these results is that many young women develop during adolescence a disorder comprised of a combination of these symptoms.

This pattern found in studies of individual symptoms is also often found in multivariate studies that have investigated which of multiple symptoms are more likely to be exhibited by females than males. Not all of the multivariate studies have reported results consonant with those discussed above but many have. Studies have found high rates among women of somatic symptoms (Dekker, Koelen, Peen, Schoevers and Gijbers van-Wijk, 2007), body image dissatisfaction, sleep problems, and fatigue (Bennett,. Ambrosini, Kudes, Metz and Rabinovich, 2005), and sleep, appetite, and pain symptoms (Lai, 2011). One item response analysis concluded that women were not more likely than men to endorse somatic symptoms (Carragher, Mewton, Slade and Teesson, 2011) but another item response analysis found gender differences in appetite/weight disturbance and fatigue (Uebelacker, Strong, Weinstock andMiller, 2009).. Two latent-trait analyses concluded that DSM depressive criteria define a single dimension (Aggen, Neale and Kendler, 2005; Muthen, 1989) but both of these studies found that the weight/appetite and fatigue criteria had the lowest loadings on the latent factor. Finally, two large reviews of many factor-analytic studies of endogenous symptoms reported that whereas most symptoms currently included in the criteria for melancholia were found to load highly on a single endogenous factor, vegetative symptoms including insomnia as well as decreased appetite and eating disturbance did not load highly on this factor (Nelson and Charney, 1981; Parker, Hadzi-Pavlovic, and Boyce, 1989).

Consonant with the hypothesized existence of a single syndrome comprised of depression and these somatic symptoms is a second similarity between studies of all of the somatic symptoms. That is, all of them have been found to be more strongly related to depression among females than among males and this pattern too develops at adolescence (e.g. eating disorders, Rodgers, Paxton and Chabrol, 2010; body dissatisfaction, Bearman and Stice, 2008; headaches, Rhee, 2000; sleep problems and fatigue, Bennett et al., 2005).

Yet another similarity among studies of all of these symptoms is that they have been shown to have increased in prevalence over recent years among young women but not, or much less so, among men (e.g. depression, Murphy et al., 2004; eating disorders, Lucas, Beard, O'Fallon and Kurland, 1991; body dissatisfaction, Cash, Morrow, Perry and Hrabosky, 2004; headaches, Manzoni, 1998; sleep problems, Santos-Silva et al., 2010; fatigue, Collishaw, Maughan, Natarajan and Pickles, 2010). This suggests the possibility that the syndrome comprised of these symptoms might be rooted in psychosocial forces related to the dramatic changes in roles experienced by women in recent decades. (Space limitations preclude the inclusion of all studies related to the patterns discussed above shared by these symptoms. Some studies do not replicate these patterns but many additional studies not cited here do, some of which are reviewed in Silverstein and Perlick, 1995).

Consonant with this hypothesis regarding changes in women's roles, the variation among cohorts over the course of most of the twentieth century has been found to be similar between the gender difference in the prevalence of depression (Silverstein and Perlick, 1991), the incidence of anorexia among young women (Lucas et al., 1991), and the correlation between scores on depression inventories and the frequency of severe headache reported by women (Silverstein, McKoy, Clauson, Perdue and Raben, 1995). These three variables that would be expected to covary if a syndrome involving all of the symptoms listed above afflicts young women, were high among cohorts born just before 1930, decreased among those born during the early 1930's, and increased again thereafter. These variations tracked historical changes in women's roles (Silverstein et al., 1991), specifically in the number of young women aspiring to educational and professional achievement who may have been distressed by the limitations that have traditionally been placed on women. The connection with women's roles will be explored more fully below.

Together, these studies point to the possibility that contemporary women exhibit higher prevalence than men of these symptoms, including depression, as a result of their exhibiting a higher prevalence of a syndrome (referred to as "somatic depression") comprised of depression and these additional somatic symptoms (Halbreich and Kahn, 2007). Should the gender difference in depressive prevalence be found to result because women exhibit more of one type of depression, somatic depression, but not of others, major implications might follow regarding the causes, treatment, and classification of depression.

Somatic depression has been found in several studies to represent much of the higher prevalence of depression among women. The original studies of somatic depression were based upon self-report data using the Center for Epidemiologic Studies Depression scale (CES-D) (Radloff, 1977) supplemented in most cases with measures of additional somatic symptoms. In these studies, somatic depression was usually defined as scoring above cutoff for depression on the CES-D and also reporting at least three of disordered eating, poor body image, insomnia, fatigue, headaches, and unexplained breathing difficulty (this last symptom was added based upon similarities between disorders described in the historical medical literature discussed below). In some studies, scoring above cutoff on an anxiety inventory was also included in the criteria. Depression in the absence of significant somatic symptoms, referred to as "pure depression", was defined as scoring above criterion for depression on the CES-D but not exhibiting enough of the somatic symptoms to meet criteria for somatic depression. These studies included samples of high school students (Silverstein, Caceres, Perdue and Cimarolli., 1995), college students (Silverstein, Clauson, Perdue, Carpman and Cimarolli, 1998), and of a reanalysis of respondents in a multi-generational sample of adults (Silverstein and Lynch, 1998). In these studies, females exhibited two-to-three times the prevalence of somatic depression as did males but little or no difference in the prevalence of pure depression (i.e. all depression other than somatic depression).

In order to improve the analysis of the relationship between gender and somatic depression, reanalyses of large epidemiologic studies that relied on research interview data were performed. These epidemiologic studies, the Epidemiologic Catchment Area Study and the National Comorbidity Survey, did not collect data from all respondents on some of the criteria included in previous studies of somatic depression, including headaches, breathing difficulty, and body image concerns, nor on specific aspects of disordered eating, such as purging. But they did collect data regarding the DSM depression criteria from all respondents who endorsed the screening item on depression. These criteria include three items that had been included in the broader criteria used in earlier studies of somatic depression, sleep and appetite disturbance and fatigue. Thus, it was possible using these large epidemiologic databases to create modified, narrower criteria for somatic depression, defined as meeting criteria for DSM major depression while exhibiting all three of these somatic symptoms.

In the ECA and NCS analyses, respondents who met these modified criteria for somatic depression were compared to those who met DSM criteria for major depression but did not also report all three of the somatic criteria, labeled as "pure depression". As in previous analyses, the gender difference in depressive prevalence was found to be primarily due to the difference in somatic depression, although the gender differences in pure depression were a bit larger using these modified criteria for somatic depression than they were using full criteria in earlier studies. Using lifetime criteria for depression, in both the ECA (Silverstein, 2002) and NCS (Silverstein, 1999) analyses, compared to men, women exhibited about one-third higher prevalence of pure depression but over twice as high a prevalence of somatic depression.

More recent analyses of representative samples in two large epidemiologic studies dealt with a weakness that may have applied to the earlier studies. That is, in all previous studies, somatic depression was defined as meeting criteria for depression plus reporting at least three additional symptoms whereas pure depression was defined as meeting criteria for depression but not meeting criteria for somatic depression without necessarily reporting any additional symptoms. Thus, the criteria for somatic depression were more stringent than those for pure depression. This leaves open the possibility that the gender difference reported resulted because women exhibited more symptoms than men, not because they exhibited depression associated with specifically somatic symptoms.

In two representative epidemiologic samples, the NCS-Replication (NCS-R)(Kessler et al., 1994) and the Zurich study (Angst, Gamma, Sellaro, Zhang and Merikangas, 2002). the gender difference in the prevalence of depression was found again to be due to the much greater prevalence among women of depression accompanied by somatic symptoms. In the NCS-R analyses, somatic depression, defined as meeting criteria for major depression while reporting all three of the somatic symptoms included in the depressive criteria, was also compared to non-somatic depression, defined as meeting major depression criteria while exhibiting at least three of the four non-somatic symptoms included in the depressive criteria. In this analysis, somatic depression was significantly related to gender among depressed respondents whereas non-somatic depression, with criteria also necessitating at least three specific depressive symptoms, was not. In the analysis of the Zurich Study, women exhibited more somatic depression than men but atypical depression, again with criteria that also necessitated at least three symptoms in addition to a diagnosis of major depression, did not add to the gender difference in depressive prevalence explained by somatic depression. These finding suggest that previous results of studies of gender differences in somatic depression were due to the somatic symptoms not simply to the greater number of symptoms and were probably not due to the overlap in criteria between somatic and atypical depression. (This possibility was tested because some studies have found that women report more atypical depression than do men and the somatic symptoms of atypical depression have been found to strongly predict the higher prevalence of depression among women) (Angst et al., 2006).

GENDER ROLES

As described above, the gender difference in depression, the incidence of anorexia among young women, and the correlation between scores on depression inventories and reports of the frequency of severe headaches among women share a similar pattern of variance over many decades of the twentieth century. Basically, these problems became more prevalent among women who matured during periods of great change in women's roles, as indexed by increases in the rates of college graduation among women. Thus, these changes involved having MORE opportunities than did the women of their mothers; generation.

The apparently paradoxical finding that problems among women are correlated with increased opportunities is understandable using a few theoretical constructs. One, encapsulated in a statement made by William James (1950) that self esteem is a function of success divided by pretensions, serves as the basis for regulatory focus theory (Higgins, 1997). This is the idea that people are more upset by failing to succeed in areas that are important to their sense of self than they are by lack of success in areas that they do not view as important. A graduate student in physics who has not done much dancing may not be bothered by being told she has two left feet but may be upset if someone questions her mathematical ability. Studies have found associations between people's reports of depression and of greater discrepancy between their aspirations in areas of importance and their perceptions of their actual characteristics and accomplishments in these areas (Papadakis and Strauman (2011). This discrepancy between actual and ideal selves has been found to be greater among girls than among boys (Hankin, Roberts and Gotlib, 1997).

In the twentieth century, increasing numbers of young girls came to aspire to achieve in areas that had traditionally been considered to be reserved for men. Many graduated college wanting to succeed in business, science, the professions and were concerned about how their intelligence and competence were viewed by others. There is little doubt that the number of women who were able to achieve in these historically nontraditional pursuits rose dramatically in recent decades. But thousands of years of attitudes toward women do not completely change in a few decades. Many of these nontraditional women continue to confront biases that make it harder for them compared to men to achieve their aspirations and to receive the respect for such achievements that men do.

Many studies demonstrate the continuing barriers faced by contemporary women who aspire to achieve outside of the traditionally feminine areas. To take just one very recent example, Moss-Racusin, Dovidio, Brescoll, Graham and Handelsman (2012) asked biology, chemistry, and physics professors to make decisions about applications allegedly submitted by undergraduate students for a position as a lab manager. All applications were identical except some were said to come from a student named John and others from a student named Jennifer. The authors found that the male student was more likely to be hired and offered mentoring, was rated as more competent, and was offered a higher salary than the female student with the identical credentials. This bias was independent of the faculty member's gender, scientific discipline, age, and tenure status. Thus, a young woman who is an aspiring physicist dealing with very difficult material is not only less likely than a young man of equal achievements to further her career by being offered a job, she is also less likely to be viewed as competent. Many contemporary young women now aspire to success in areas once reserved for men but continue to face limitations not only in opportunities but also in the respect accorded to them for their achievements. These limitations may be exacerbated in adulthood if parents begin to place pressure primarily on their daughters and daughters-in-law to give up time devoted to work in order to give birth to grandchildren or if, as is most common, mothers take more time from careers than fathers to deal with children.

Some of the earliest indications of gender limitations that girls may receive may come from members of their families. These might include fathers who indicate that they think boys are more important than girls, brothers who receive more privileges or have less rigid restrictions, such as curfews, applied to them than sisters, mothers whose jobs are treated as less important than those of fathers, and observations of mothers suggesting that the mothers have experienced their lives as being limited by their being female. These and other behaviors indicative of gender-role-limitations may vary greatly from family to family and may be less frequent than they once were, but they may continue to be exhibited in many families. These behaviors in the family are reinforced by behaviors girls observe in school (boys picking on girls, smart girls not being as popular) and the media (Superman-type characters continue to save Lois Lane-type characters more than vice versa, no President of the United States has yet been female). Together these observations may lead many young women, perhaps not always with full awareness, to come to feel that being female leads them to be seen as "lesser".

One way of describing this process is to say that as they are growing up, many contemporary girls may develop self-schemas (Markus, 1977) as competent people full of opportunities based upon their achievement in school, sports skills, encouraging words from teachers or coaches, and the general notion that girls nowadays should be able to do anything. At the same time, the girls may begin to develop gender schemas (Bem, 1981) that females are at a disadvantage based upon observations such as those described above. It may be at adolescence, when they begin to develop the curves and secondary sex characteristics of women, that girls come to be treated differently by many people than they were before. Their gender schemas may come into increasing contact with their self schemas and their feelings of opportunity and pride may confront those of limitation due to being female. Processes such as these may help to explain the great jump in depressive feelings exhibited by girls at adolescence and the development of somatic depression at this time.

Several studies have found an association between somatic depression and gender-role-limitations reported by young women in high school and college. Somatic depression has been found to be significantly related to women's reports of feeling limited by societal responses to their gender, of viewing their mothers' lives as having been limited by their mothers' gender, and of viewing their fathers as exhibiting a preference for males (Silverstein, Caceres et al., 1995; Silverstein, Clauson et al., 1998). Furthermore, women's reports of somatic depression have also been found to be related to reports made by their parents regarding gender roles that may have led to the development of negative gender schemas, including fathers' attitudes that women should not have authority over men and mothers' reports of believing that their own achievements were limited by their gender (Silverstein and Blumenthal, 1997; Silverstein and Lynch, 1998). In all of these studies, women's reports of pure depression were not found to be related to reports made either by the women or by their parents regarding gender roles.

In one study (Silverstein et al., 1997), mothers' reports of having felt limited by their gender were significantly related to their daughters' reports of somatic depression, but not to the daughters' reports of pure depression. In fascinating contrast, mothers' self-reports of depression were found to be significantly related to daughters' reports of pure depression but not (once mothers' reports of gender-role limitations were factored out) to daughters' reports of somatic depression. Although this finding needs to be replicated, it suggests that while somatic depression may be rooted in part in responses to gender-role limitations, pure depression may be rooted in more endogenous factors. This possibility becomes more intriguing in light of recent analyses of the STAR*D Study (Silverstein and Patel, 2011) that found poorer response to antidepressant medication among patients exhibiting somatic depression compared to those exhibiting pure depression. This pattern of findings on gender roles, maternal depression, and response to antidepressants points to the possibility that somatic and pure depression might best be considered distinct disorders rather than merely two phenotypes of a single disorder, major depression. If that is the case, then we might conclude that a distinct disorder, somatic depression, has been subsumed within the criteria of a diagnosis, major depressive disorder, received by large numbers of women.

This possibility should be viewed in the light of findings from the history of psychiatry. Over the centuries, several diagnoses that involved symptoms quite similar to those discussed here were described in the medical literature as afflicting young woman. While some of the patients who received these diagnoses exhibited different symptoms, the lists of symptoms were large enough to include people suffering from what is termed here somatic depression. Common symptoms of the disorder chlorosis included depression, nervousness, headaches, breathing difficulties, insomnia, anorexia, bulimia, and vomiting (Allbutt,1901; Laycock, 1840). Included in lists of the common symptoms of the disease neurasthenia were nervous depression, headaches, insomnia, asthma, and emaciation (Deale and Adams, 1894; Lutz, 1991). Over 60 percent of a sample of hysteric women were reported to exhibit anorexia, vomiting, nervousness, symptoms of depression, headaches, and breathing difficulties. (Purtell, Robins and Cohen, 1951).

In the 19th century, when women first began to pursue higher education, these diagnoses became extremely common, Chlorosis was so commonly diagnosed among young women that one authority wrote that perhaps every girl passes through chlorosis in the process of maturing (Allbutt, 1901). One doctor noted that during adolescence symptoms of hysteria are the rule. (Mercier cited in Showalter, 1985). Those afflicted with these disorders were often young women who, rather than restrict themselves to the traditional roles prescribed for the women of their day, were striving for higher education. In the words of two physicians writing about neurasthenia, the disease arose out of "the natural nervous tendency of a young girl or woman harassed by the ambitions of school life . . . or annoyed with household and family chores" (Deale et al., 1894, p. 190). Given the prejudices of their times, doctors explained these patterns using the construct of mental strain – it was unhealthy for women to expend energy on learning just when their complex reproductive systems were developing during puberty. Mental strain was noted in the literature as a cause of chlorosis, neurasthenia, and hysteria (Simon, 1897; Gosling, 1987; Preston, 1897).

Thus, when women's roles began to expand for some, as indexed by the earliest generations of female college students, disorders involving depression, disordered eating, headaches, insomnia, fatigue, and breathing difficulties were described in the medical literature as becoming prevalent among adolescent women. It is likely that while differences existed between these disorders, enough similarities existed to allow young women faced with gender-role-limitations who exhibited the symptoms discussed here to receive the diagnoses popular at their time. Given the studies reviewed above, many contemporary young women in similar circumstances may be being diagnosed with major depression rather than what may be a distinct disorder.

REFERENCES

Abu-Arefeh, I., and Russell, G. (1994). Prevalence of headache and migraine in schoolchildren. *British Medical Journal, 309,* 765-769.

Aggen SH, Neale MC Kendler K S (2005). DSM Criteria for major depression: evaluating symptom patterns using latent-trait item response models. Psychol Med 35:475-487.

Allbutt, T. C. (1901). Clorosis. In T. C. Allbutt (Ed.) *A system of medicine by many authors, Vol. V.* New York: Macmillan, 481-518.

Angst, J., Gamma, A., Benazzi, F., Silverstein, B., Ajdacic-Gross, V., Eich, D., and Rossler, W. (2006). Atypical depressive syndromes in varying definitions. E*uropean Archive of Psychiatric and Clinical Neuroscience, 256,* 44-54.

Angst, J., Gamma, A., Sellaro, R., Zhang, H., and Merikangas, K. (2002). Toward validation of atypical depression in the community: Results of the Zurich cohort study. *Journal of Affective Disorders, 72,* 125-138.

Bearman, S. K. and Stice, E. (2008). Testing a gender additive model: The role of body image in adolescent depression. *Journal of Abnormal Child Psychology, 36,* 1251-1263.

Bem, S. L. (1981). Gender schema theory: A cognitive account of sextyping. *Psychological Review, 88,* 354-364.

Bennett, D. S., Ambrosini, P. J., Kudes, D., Metz, C., and Rabinovich, H. (2005). Gender differences in adolescent depression: Do symptoms differ for boys and girls? *Journal of Affective Disorders, 89,* 35-44.

Carragher N, Mewton L Slade T Teesson M (2011). An item response analysis of the DSM-IV criteria for major depression: Findings from the Australian National Survey of Mental Health and Wellbeing. *Journal of Affective Disorders*, 130(1-2):92-8.

Cash, T. F., Morrow, J. A., Perry, A. A., and Hrabosky, J. (2004). How has body image changed? A cross-sectional investigatin of college women and men from 1983 to 2001. *Journal of Consulting and Clinical Psychology, 72,* 1081-1089.

Collishaw, S., Maughan, B., Natarajan, L., and Pickles, A. (2010). Trends in adolescent emotional problems in England: a comparison of two national cohorts twenty years apart. *Journal of Child Psychology and Psychiatry, 51,* 885-894.

Deale, H. B. and Adams, S. S. (1894). Neurasthenia in young women. *American Journal of Obstetrics,* 29, 190-195.

Dekker J Koelen JA Peen J Schoevers RA Gijbers van-Wijk C (2007). Gender differences in clinical features of depressed outpatients: preliminary evidence for subtyping of depression? Women Health, 46:19-38.

Ge, X., Conger, R. D., and Elder, G. H. (2001). Pubertal transition, stressful life events, and the emergence of gender differences in adolescent depressive symptoms. *Developmental Psychology, 37,* 404-417.

Gosling, F. G. (1987). *Before Freud: Neurasthenia and the American medical community, 1870-1910.* Urbana: University of Illinois Press.

Halbreich, U., and Kahn, L. S. 2007). Atypical depression, somatic depression and anxious depression in women: Are they gender-preferred phenotypes? *Journal of Affective Disorders*, 102, 245–258.

Hankin, B. I., Roberts, J. and Gotlib, I. H. (1997). Elevated self-standards and emotional distress during adolescence: Emotional specificity and gender differences. *Cognitive Therapyand Research,* 21, 663-679.

Higgins, E. T. (1997). Beyond pleasure and pain. *American Psychologist,* 52, 1280-1300.

James, W. (1950). *The principles of psychology, Vol. I.* New York: Dover.

Johnson, E. O., Roth, T., Schultz, L., and Breslau, N. (2006). Epidemiology of DSM-IV insomnia in adolescence: Lifetime prevalence, chronicity, and an emergent gender difference. *Pediatrics, 117,* e247-256.

Kessler, R. C., Mcgonagle, K. A., Zhao, S., Nelson, C. B., Hughes, M., Eshleman, S., et al. (1994). Lifetime and 12-month prevalence of *DSM-III-R* psychiatric disorders in the United States: Results from the National Comorbidity Survey. *Archives of General Psychiatry*, *51*, 8–19.

Lai C (2011). Major depressive disorder: gender differences in symptoms, life quality, and sexual function. Clin Psychopharm 31:39-44.

Laycock, T. (1840). *An essay on hysteria.* Philadelphia: Haswell, Barrington and Haswell.

Ledoux, S., Choquet, M., and Flament, M. (1991). Eating disorders among adolescents in an unselected French population. *International Journal of Eating Disorders, 10,* 81-89.

Lucas, A. R., Beard, C. M., O'Fallon, W. M., and Kurland, L. T. (1991). 50-year trends in the incidence of anorexia nervosa in Rochester, Minn.: a population-based study. *American Journal of Psychiatry, 148,* 917-922.

Lutz, T. (1991). *American nervousness, 1903.* Ithaca, N. Y.: Cornell University Press.

Mancilla-Diaz, J. M., Lopez-Aguilar, X., Franco-Paredes, K., Alvarez-Rayon, G., Vazquez-Aravalo, R., and Trinidad Ocampo Tellez-Giron, M. (2009). Effect of gender and school level on disordered eating behaviours and attitudes in Mexcian adolescents. *Eating and Weight Disorders, 14,* e169-175.

Manzoni, G. C. (1998). Gender ratio of cluster headache over the years: a possible role of changes in lifestyle. *Cephalalgia, 18,* 138-142.

Markus, H. (1977). Self-schemata and processing information about the self. *Journal of Personality and Social Psychology, 35,* 63-78.

Moss-Racusin, C. A., Dovidio, J. F., Brescoll, V. L., Graham, M. J. and Handelsman, J. (2012). *Science faculty's subtle* gender *biases favor male students. Proceedings of the National Academy of Sciences of the United States of America.* 109 (41), 16474-16479.

Murphy, J. M., Horton, N. J., Laird, N. M., Monroe, R. R., Sobol, A. M., and Leighton, A. H. (2004). Anxiety and depression: a 40-year perspective on relationships regarding prevalence, distribution, and comorbidity. *Acta Psychiatrica Scandinavica, 309,* 355-375.

Muthen, B. O. (1989). Dichotomous factor analysis of symptoms data. *Sociology Methods Research,* 18, 19-65.

Nelson, J. C. and.Charney, D.S. (1981). The symptoms of major depressive illness. *American Journal of Psychiatry,* 138, 1-13.

Papadakis, A. A. and Strauman, T. J. (2011). Stress, coping, socialization, and goals: A self-regulation perspective on gender and depression in adolescence. In T. J. Strauman, P. R. Costanzo and J. Garber (Eds.), *Depression in Adolescent Girls.* New York: Guilford Press, 151-190.

Parker, G., Hadzi-Pavlovic, D. and Boyce, P. (1989). Endogenous depression as a construct: a quantitative analysis of the literature and a study of clinician judgements. *Australia and New Zealand Journal of Psychiatry.* 23, 357-368.

Preston, G. J. (1907). *Hysteria and certain allied conditions.* Philadelphia: P. Blakiston.

Purtell, J. J., Robins, E. and Cohen, M. E. (1951). Observations on clinical aspects of hysteria. *Journal of the American Medical Association,* 146, 902-910.

Radloff, L. S. (1977). The CES-D scale: a self-report depression scale for research in the general population. *Applied Psychological Measurement, 1, 385-401.*

Rhee, H. (2000). Prevalence and predictors of headaches in US adolescents. *Headache, 40, 528-538.*

Rodgers, R. F., Paxton, S. J., and Chabrol, H. (2010). Depression as a moderator of sociocultural influences on eating disorder symptoms in adolescent females and males. *Journal of Youth and Adolescence, 39, 393-402.*

Santos-Silva, R., Bettencourt, L. R. A., Pires, M. L. N., de Mello, M. T., Taddei J. A., Benedito-Silva, A. A. et al., (2010). Increasing trends of sleep complaints in the city of Sao Paulo, Brazil. *Sleep Medicine, 11,* 520-524.

Showalter, E. (1985). *The female malady: Women, madness and English culture, 1830-1980.* New York: Pantheon.

Silverstein B. and Perlick D. (1995). The Cost of Competence. New York, Oxford University Press.

Silverstein, B. (1999). Gender difference in the prevalence of clinical depression: the role played by depression associated with somatic symptoms. *American Journal of Psychiatry, 156,* 480–482.

Silverstein, B. (2002). Gender Differences in the Prevalence of Somatic Versus Pure Depression: A Replication, *American Journal of Psychiatry, 159,* 1051-1052.

Silverstein., B and Blumenthal, E. (1997). Depression mixed with anxiety, somatization, and disordered eating: relationship with gender role-related limitations experienced by females. *Sex Roles, 36,* 709–724.

Silverstein, B., Caceres, J., Perdue, L., and Cimarolli, V (1995). Gender differences in depressive symptomatology: the role played by "anxious somatic depression" associated with gender-related achievement concerns. *Sex Roles, 33,* 621–636.

Silverstein, B., Clauson, J., Perdue, L., Carpman, S., and Cimarolli, V. (1998). The association between female college students' reports of depression and their perceptions of parental attitudes regarding gender. *Journal of Applied Social Psychology, 28,* 537–549.

Silverstein, B., and Lynch, A. D. (1998). Gender differences in depression: the role played by paternal attitudes of male superiority and maternal modeling of gender-related limitations. *Sex Roles, 38,* 539–556.Silverstein, B., McKoy, E., Clauson, J., Perdue, L., and Raben, J. (1995). The correlation between depression and headache: The role played by generational changes in female achievement. *Journal of Applied Social Psychology, 25,* 35-48.

Silverstein, B. and Patel, P. (2010). Poor response to antidepressant medication of patients with somatic depression in the STAR*D Study. *Psychiatry Research,* 187 (1-2), 121-124.

Silverstein, B. and Perlick, D. (1991). Gender differences in depression: Historical changes. *Acta Psychiatrica Scandinavica, 84,* 327-331.

Simon, J. (1897). A study of chlorosis. *American Journal of Medical Science,* 113, 349-423.

ter Wolbeek, M., van Doornen, L. J. P., Kavelaars, A. and Heijnen, C. J. (2006). Severe fatigue in adolescents: A common phenomenon? *Pediatrics, 117,* e1078-1086.

Uebelacker LA Strong D Weinstock LM Miller W (2009). Use of item response theory to understand differential functioning of DSM-IV major depression symptoms by race, ethnicity and gender. Psychol Med 39: 591-601.

INDEX

B

C

D

E

F

G

H

I

J

K

L

M

Q

R

S

T

U

V

W

Y